INTELLECTUAL PROPERTY IN THE 21ST CENTURY

DOJ PROGRESS REPORT ON INTELLECTUAL PROPERTY

INTELLECTUAL PROPERTY IN THE 21ST CENTURY

Additional books in this series can be found on Nova's website at:

https://www.novapublishers.com/catalog/index.php?cPath=23_29&seriesp=Intellectual+Property+in+the+21st+Century

Additional E-books in this series can be found on Nova's website at:

https://www.novapublishers.com/catalog/index.php?cPath=23_29&seriespe=Intellectual+Property+in+the+21st+Century

INTELLECTUAL PROPERTY IN THE 21ST CENTURY

DOJ PROGRESS REPORT ON INTELLECTUAL PROPERTY

TODD B. PARKER
EDITOR

Nova Science Publishers, Inc.
New York

For permission to use material from this book please contact us:
Telephone 631-231-7269; Fax 631-231-8175
Web Site: http://www.novapublishers.com

LIBRARY OF CONGRESS CATALOGING-IN-PUBLICATION DATA

DOJ progress report on intellectual property / editor, Todd B. Parker.
p. cm.
Includes index.
ISBN 978-1-60741-001-0 (hardcover)
1.Intellectual property--United States--Criminal provisions. I. Parker, Todd B. (Todd Benjamin), 1952- II. United States. Dept. of Justice. III. United States. Department of Justice's Task Force on Intellectual Property. Report of the Department of Justice's Task Force on Intellectual Property. IV. Title: Department of Justice progress report on intellectual property.
KF9359.D65 2010
345.73'0266--dc22
2010016685

Published by Nova Science Publishers, Inc. ✦ New York

CONTENTS

PREFACE

The Attorney General directed the Task Force to examine all of the Department of Justice's intellectual property enforcement efforts and to explore ways for the Department of Justice to increase its protection of valuable intellectual property resources. The Attorney General formed a team of legal experts with a diverse range of experience and expertise to examine this important area of the law. The Task Force analyzed existing resources and proposed significant improvements in the following areas: criminal enforcement; international cooperation; civil enforcement; antitrust enforcement; legislation; and prevention. This book explores the topic of intellectual property theft and its rising threat against our nation's economic security.

This is an edited, reformatted and augmented version of a U. S. Department of Justice publication dated June 2006.

MESSAGE FROM THE CHAIRMAN

"Theft of intellectual property threatens America's economic prosperity and the health, safety, and security of its citizens." - D. Kyle Sampson, Chairman, Intellectual Property Task Force

Intellectual property is America's competitive advantage in the global economy of the 21st century. From music and movies to pharmaceuticals and software, intellectual property touches every aspect of our lives. Theft of intellectual property threatens America's economic prosperity and the health, safety, and security of its citizens. Accordingly, the Bush Administration has launched the most aggressive, ambitious, and far-reaching law enforcement effort ever taken against intellectual property crimes and related civil misconduct. This Progress Report of the Department of Justice's Task Force on Intellectual Property sets forth the significant accomplishments of the Department of Justice in this unprecedented law enforcement effort. The accomplishments were made possible by the support of President Bush and Attorney General Gonzales, both of whom recognize the importance of intellectual property and have committed new resources to its protection. And these achievements are also the result of the dedicated efforts of career investigators, civil enforcers, and criminal prosecutors who combat misappropriation and intellectual property offenses every day. I express thanks to the members and executive staff of the Task Force, as well as to the other contributors, for their work in preparing this Progress Report. They are leading the charge to protect intellectual property and keep our Nation safe and prosperous. D. Kyle Sampson Chairman

In: DOJ Progress Report on Intellectual Property ISBN: 978-1-60741-001-0
Editor: Todd B. Parker

Chapter 1

INTRODUCTION

Department of Justice

Counterfeit products and the theft of intellectual property have real-world consequences. Not only is intellectual property theft a threat to our economy, but it also can be a serious threat to our health and safety. Counterfeit batteries can explode, counterfeit car parts can fail to perform, and counterfeit pharmaceuticals can lack the ingredients necessary to cure deadly diseases.

The Department of Justice takes the problem of intellectual property theft very seriously. The Attorney General has made protecting and enforcing intellectual property rights one of the Department of Justice's highest priorities, and implementing the recommendations in the 2004 Report has been an urgent mission. (A listing of all of the recommendations can be found in *Appendix A*). The Department of Justice is proud to announce that it has implemented all of the recommendations contained in the 2004 Report, including:

- Increasing the number of prosecutors in the field by creating five additional Computer Hacking and Intellectual Property ("CHIP") Units in:
  - the District of Columbia
  - Nashville, Tennessee
  - Orlando, Florida
  - Pittsburgh, Pennsylvania

  - Sacramento, California
- Deploying an experienced federal prosecutor as an Intellectual Property Law Enforcement Coordinator ("IPLEC") to southeast Asia and obtaining funding for an IPLEC in Eastern Europe to handle regional efforts to enforce and protect intellectual property;
- Dismantling international criminal organizations that commit intellectual property offenses;
- Expanding international training and technical assistance efforts;
- Increasing the number of extradition and mutual legal assistance treaties that include intellectual property offenses;
- Prosecuting intellectual property cases involving a threat to public health and safety;
- Carefully monitoring and vigorously protecting the right of victims to pursue intellectual property cases in civil courts;
- Organizing victims' conferences on intellectual property awareness; and
- Creating innovative intellectual property educational programs for America's youth.

The Department of Justice did not stop at simply implementing the recommendations of the Task Force. Instead, the Department of Justice went well beyond the recommendations by taking these additional steps:

- Creating seven additional CHIP Units in:
  - Austin, Texas
  - Baltimore, Maryland
  - Denver, Colorado
  - Detroit, Michigan
  - Newark, New Jersey
  - New Haven, Connecticut
  - Philadelphia, Pennsylvania
- Increasing the number of defendants prosecuted for intellectual property offenses by 98 percent;
- Transmitting to Congress the President's Intellectual Property Protection Act of 2005;
- Providing training and technical assistance to over 2,000 foreign prosecutors, investigators, and judges regarding intellectual property investigations and prosecutions;

- Working with the United States Trade Representative to improve language regarding intellectual property protections in Free Trade Agreements and other international treaties;
- Publishing a nearly 400-page comprehensive resource manual on prosecuting intellectual property crimes;
- Filing 13 *amicus,* or "friend of the court," briefs in the Supreme Court in cases involving intellectual property disputes; and
- Partnering with the United States Patent & Trademark Office to dedicate $900,000 over three years for piracy prevention efforts with non-profit educational institutions.

As can be seen from these achievements, the Department of Justice has made intellectual property enforcement and protection a high priority. The following Progress Report chronicles these achievements and important goals.

Attorney General Alberto R. Gonzales at the United States Capitol in Washington, DC. Photo by Craig Crawford.

"[W]e recognize our responsibility to vigorously enforce IP laws–and develop a culture of respect for IP rights–in order to harness America's creative energy and ingenuity for the future of our economy."

- Attorney General Alberto R. Gonzales, March 22, 2006

In: DOJ Progress Report on Intellectual Property ISBN: 978-1-60741-001-0
Editor: Todd B. Parker

Chapter 2

WHAT IS INTELLECTUAL PROPERTY?

Department of Justice

America is built upon human innovation and creativity. People, inspired by artistic visions or new ideas, create movies for us to watch, music for us to hear, and books for us to read. Inventors and creators develop products that improve our lives. Whether they produce music, design fashion, or develop chemical compounds, inventors and creators contribute their intellect and ideas for our Nation's benefit.

Just as the law grants ownership rights over our material possessions, such as a home or an automobile, it also grants individuals ownership rights over intangible property, such as an idea or an invention. When a person creates something novel and unique, our laws recognize its value and grant the creator the respect and integrity of ownership.

The Constitution itself recognizes that intellectual property protection is an important factor in fostering innovation and creativity. Article I, Section 8 states that Congress shall have the power:

> To promote the Progress of Science and useful Arts, by securing for limited Times to Authors and Inventors the exclusive Right to their respective Writings and Discoveries.

U.S. Const. Art. I, § 8. Reflecting the diversity of intellectual property, there are distinct areas of the law that protect it: copyrights; trademarks, service marks, and certification marks; trade secrets; and patents.

COPYRIGHTS

Books, music, movies, artwork, and plays, among other creative works, can all be protected by copyrights. With certain exceptions, the owner of a copyright holds exclusive control over various rights associated with his or her works, such as the rights to reproduce, publicly distribute, publicly display, publicly perform, rent, record, or adapt the work. The protection lasts for a limited period of time, usually 70 years after the author's death.

Copyrights protect any creative work that is original and tangibly expressed. Although the physical expression of an idea is protected, the actual idea is not. Thus, facts presented in a work are freely available to the public, so long as the exact manner of expression is not copied. This allows society to benefit from the accessibility of facts and ideas themselves, while still protecting the original creative works that present those facts and ideas.

Copyright protection applies as soon as the work is expressed in a concrete form, without any need for the creator to apply for a copyright. A copyright owner, however, can register the work with the United States Copyright Office to create a public record of the creation.

TRADEMARKS, SERVICE MARKS, AND CERTIFICATION MARKS

In addition to protecting creative works, intellectual property law protects trademarks, service marks, and certification marks. A trademark is any trait used to identify and distinguish a product or its producer. A service mark is any trait used to identify and distinguish a service. For example, McDonald's golden arches design is a commonly recognized service mark and the Nike "swoosh" is a well-known trademark; both immediately identify the companies they represent. A certification mark is a mark used to certify regional or other origin, material, mode of manufacturer, quality, accuracy or other characteristics of goods or services. An example of a certification mark includes Underwriters Laboratories' "UL" mark, which certifies the safety standards of electrical equipment.

Trademarks and service marks convey the integrity and uniqueness of a product or service by allowing a consumer to distinguish one product or service from another. The mark may be part of the item or its packaging, and may include a distinctive symbol, word, name, sign, shape, or color. Even sounds and smells may be part of a mark. Generic terms like "soap," however, do not qualify as marks.

Manufacturers that have developed a good brand image and a reputation of high quality should be able to rely on their marks to prevent others from capitalizing on their success, and to ensure that customers can easily identify and purchase their products or services. Trademarks and service marks, therefore, contribute to fair competition in the marketplace. Consumers, in turn, rely on trademarks and service marks to differentiate between products and services, and select those associated with reputations they trust.

Registering a mark with the United States Patent and Trademark Office ("USPTO") confers important advantages on the mark owner. For example, the owner can obtain the exclusive right to use the mark in the United States and can exclude others from using the mark, or a comparable mark, in a way that would confuse consumers. Marks also are protected by anti-dilution laws, which ensure that a famous mark's distinctiveness cannot be blurred by the commercial actions of others, even if those actions fall just short of causing confusion. Federal trademark and service mark registration is necessary for federal criminal prosecutions for trafficking in counterfeit goods or services.

In order to register a trademark with the USPTO, the applicant must demonstrate that (1) the mark is distinctive, and (2) the mark will be used, or is intended for use, in interstate or foreign commerce. A trade-mark, service mark, or certification mark generally does not expire as long as it continues to be used.

Trade Secrets

A trade secret is any confidential information used by a business that has some independent economic value and that is kept secret by those who possess it. The recipes for Coca-Cola and Pepsi, for example, are protected trade secrets. Trade secrets include scientific, technological, or business information, such as marketing strategies, and even information on "what-not-to-do," such as failed or defective inventions. When the once-secret information is obtained through legitimate means, however, it can be freely used. For example, trade secret protection does not prevent a scientist who reverse-engineers a product and discovers how it is assembled from legally using that information to re-create the product. Furthermore, trade secret protection applies only while secrecy is maintained. After the trade secret is publicly disclosed, it loses its legal protection against future disclosure.

Patents

The final major category of protected intellectual property is patents. From the composition of a new drug to the latest time-saving gadget, patents protect the world of inventions. They provide an exclusive right to the fruits of an invention for 20 years from the date the patent application is filed. In return, the patent applicant must agree to publicly disclose the basis for the invention, so that other members of the public may use the information freely to develop new products or ideas. The patent statutes do not necessarily permit all inventions to be patented; for instance, a patent will not be awarded for discoveries that are not novel or that are obvious. Laws of nature and natural phenomena, such as gravity and acceleration, also are not eligible for patent protection because they are not human creations. The United States has numerous international agreements with foreign countries to protect patents and, although there are no federal criminal laws prohibiting the infringement of patents, federal civil laws allow owners of patents to file lawsuits in United States courts.

In: DOJ Progress Report on Intellectual Property ISBN: 978-1-60741-001-0
Editor: Todd B. Parker

Chapter 3

WHAT LAWS PROTECT INTELLECTUAL PROPERTY?

Department of Justice

Since Congress enacted the first criminal law protecting copyright in 1897, the federal government's role in enforcing intellectual property rights has evolved to reflect the changing technologies and media of expression and distribution. The Internet and other technologies have revolutionized the ability to misappropriate information and have made intellectual property infringement a global problem affecting all nations.

At the same time as intellectual property has become increasingly more critical for the economic security of the United States, misappropriating intellectual property has become easier. Unfortunately, the consequences have become more devastating: people are deceived, property is stolen, and businesses are harmed. Federal laws that criminalize violations of intellectual property rights, just like other criminal laws that aim to protect property, deter fraud, and encourage market stability, are important to the safety and prosperity of America and its citizens.

As noted above, federal law protects four categories of intellectual property: copyrighted works; trademarks, service marks, and certification marks; trade secrets; and patents. A summary of the federal laws protecting these types of intellectual property follows.

Protection of Copyrighted Works

Federal criminal copyright law protects against the unauthorized use of copyrighted works. Prohibited uses include the unauthorized copying and distribution of copyrighted works, such as books, films, musical compositions, sound recordings, software programs, and artistic works. A business that willfully makes and sells unauthorized copies of copyrighted motion pictures, for example, is committing a federal crime.

Many copyrighted works contain technology intended to hinder the copying of the work by persons not authorized to do so. Federal criminal copyright law prohibits willfully creating or selling technology to circumvent such protections. Disabling embedded codes that protect computer software from unauthorized copying, for example, may violate federal law. In certain circumstances, it is also a violation of federal criminal law to willfully distribute goods or services, for commercial purposes, that disable those defenses.

Federal law provides additional protection for copyrighted works that falls outside criminal copyright law. For example, trafficking in counterfeit labels that are, or are designed to be, attached to copyrighted works is prohibited. Additionally, copyright owners may sue copyright infringers under federal copyright law.

"Our effort to combat the growing trend of high-tech crimes includes a robust enforcement of the laws protecting intellectual property."

- Attorney General Alberto R. Gonzales, March 22, 2006

Protection of Trademarks, Service Marks, and Certification Marks

Federal criminal law protects trademarks, service marks, and certification marks against infringement. For instance, it is a federal crime to knowingly traffic in goods or services that bear a counterfeit mark if the actual mark has been properly registered. This law protects not only mark owners, but also consumers, who might otherwise be led to pay a premium for goods or services they think are from a reputable mark owner only to receive imitations of lesser quality. Some counterfeit goods can create serious risks to consumer health and safety, such as counterfeit pharmaceuticals that have a chemical composition or purity different than the genuine drug. In addition, an electrical cord bearing a counterfeit UL certification mark may be substandard and catch fire.

Mark owners may also bring private lawsuits under federal law for infringement, even if the Department of Justice does not file criminal charges.

PROTECTION OF TRADE SECRETS

Federal criminal laws also protect trade secrets. It is thus a federal crime to misappropriate intentionally a trade secret for the purpose of benefitting a foreign government or for economic gain. For example, federal law may prohibit an employee of a soft drink company from providing to a competitor the secret recipe for his employer's product. Likewise, an engineer might commit a federal offense if he were to provide his company's confidential research results to a competitor or foreign power.

PATENTS

Federal law protects patents by providing for their exclusive registration by the USPTO and by providing patent owners with a civil cause of action to enjoin future infringement and to recover damages for past infringement. Federal law also provides for the plaintiff in a patent case to recover three times the damages suffered for past infringement in some circumstances.

A developer of intellectual property often has a choice of whether to protect an invention by patenting it or by deeming it a trade secret. Each of these forms of intellectual property has advantages and disadvantages. For instance, although patents convey a range of benefits, patents require that the applicant disclose to the public the elements of the patented invention, and a patent lasts for only 20 years. By contrast, a trade secret, by definition, is not disclosed and may last indefinitely. In addition, while stealing a trade secret may violate federal criminal statutes, there are no criminal laws regarding patent infringement.

Other Laws

Various other laws protect intellectual property in particular situations. For instance, federal criminal law prohibits knowingly recording live musical performances and copying and distributing those recordings for profit. In addition, it is a federal offense to willfully infringe a copyright by distributing without authorization, over publicly-available computer networks, certain copyrighted works–including movies, software, and music–before their release date. Federal laws can also be violated when devices are manufactured or distributed that permit the interception of cable or satellite television signals or the descrambling of satellite television signals. Moreover, several international agreements exist to coordinate copyright and other intellectual property protections.

Federal Criminal Laws Protecting Intellectual Property

Copyright

17 U.S.C. § 506(a)(1)(A) [(formerly § 506(a)(1))] & 18 U.S.C. § 2319(b)

Copyright Infringement for Profit (Felony)

Statutory maximum penalty of 5 years in prison and a $250,000 fine or twice the gain/loss for an indi-vidual first-time offender (10 years for second offense); $500,000 fine or twice the gain/loss for a corporate offender. Civil and criminal forfeiture available.

17 U.S.C. § 506(a)(1)(B) [(formerly § 506(a)(2))] & 18 U.S.C. § 2319(c)

Large-Scale Copyright Infringement Without Profit Motive (Felony)

Statutory maximum penalty of 3 years in prison and $250,000 fine or twice the gain/loss for an individual first-time offender (6 years for second offense); $500,000 fine or twice gain/loss for corporate offend-er. Civil and criminal forfeiture available.

17 U.S.C. § 506(a)(1)(C) & 18 U.S.C. § 2319(d)

Distribution of Pre-Release Copyrighted Works or Material over Publicly-Accessible Computer Network

If infringement is effected for commercial purpose: Statutory maximum penalty of 5 years in prison and a $250,000 fine or twice the gross gain/loss for an indi- vidual first-time offender (10 years for second offense); $500,000 fine or twice the gain/loss for a corporate offender. Civil and criminal forfeiture available.

If infringement is not effected for commercial purpose: Statutory maximum penalty of 3 years in prison and $250,000 fine or twice the gain/loss for an individual first-time offender (6 years for second offense); $500,000 fine or twice the gain/loss for a corporate offender. Civil and criminal forfeiture available.

17 U.S.C. § 1204

Technology to Circumvent Anti-Piracy Protections Digital Millennium Copyright Act ("DMCA")

Statutory maximum penalty of 5 years in prison and a $500,000 fine or twice the gain/loss for an individual and corporate first-time offender. Statutory maximum penalty of 10 years in prison for a second offense and a $1 million dollars fine or twice the gain/loss. No for-feiture available.

18 U.S.C. § 2318

Counterfeit/Illicit Labels and Counterfeit Documentation and Packaging for Copyrighted Works

Statutory maximum penalty of 5 years in prison and a $250,000 fine or twice the gross gain/loss for an indi-vidual; $500,000 fine or twice the gain/loss for a cor-porate offender. Criminal and civil forfeiture available.

18 U.S.C. § 2319A

Bootleg Recordings of Live Musical Performances

Statutory maximum penalty of 5 years in prison and a $250,000 fine or twice the gain/loss for an individual first-time offender (10 years for second offense); $500,000 or twice the gain/loss for a cor-porate offender. Civil and criminal forfeiture available.

18 U.S.C. § 2319B

Camcording

Statutory maximum penalty of 3 years in prison and $250,000 fine or twice the gain/loss for an individual first-time offender (6 years for second offense); $500,000 fine or twice the gain/loss for a corporate offender. Criminal forfeiture available.

Trademarks, Service Marks, and Certification Marks

18 U.S.C. § 2320

Counterfeit Trademarks, Service Marks, and Certifi-cation Marks

Statutory maximum penalty of 10 years in prison and a $2 million fine or twice the gain/loss for an individual first-time offender; $5 million fine or twice the gain/loss for corporate offender. For second-time offenders statutory maximum penalty of 20 years in prison and a $5 million fine or twice the gain/loss for an individual; $15 million fine or twice the gain/loss for corporate offender. Civil and criminal forfeiture available.

Trade Secrets

18 U.S.C. § 1831

Economic Espionage to Benefit a Foreign Government

Statutory maximum of 15 years in prison and a $500,000 fine or twice the gain/loss for an individual offender, $10 million fine or twice the gain/loss for a corporate offender. Criminal forfeiture is available.

18 U.S.C. § 1832

Commercial Theft of Trade Secrets

Statutory maximum penalty of 10 years in prison and a $250,000 fine or twice the gain/loss for an individual first-time offender (10 years for second offense); $5 million fine or twice the gain/loss for a corporate offender. Criminal forfeiture available.

In: DOJ Progress Report on Intellectual Property ISBN: 978-1-60741-001-0
Editor: Todd B. Parker

Chapter 4

WHY IS PROTECTING INTELLECTUAL PROPERTY RIGHTS IMPORTANT?

Department of Justice

In our 21st century economy, intellectual property is one of the most valuable forms of property that exists. Whether it is the copyright of a blockbuster film, a patent on a breakthrough drug, a trade secret relating to an innovative product, or a trademark on one of the world's most valuable brands, intellectual property is a significant source of the growth of the American economy and a key driver of global economic activity. As America and more countries around the world move from an industrial to an information-based economy, the importance of protecting intellectual property will only continue to increase.

> *"[T]he strength of the American economy is dependent on the creative and entrepreneurial spirit of our citizens. At the heart of that spirit is the dedicated protection of intellectual property – and the innovations, jobs, and productivity that flow from it."*
>
> \- Attorney General Alberto R. Gonzales, March 22, 2006

The negative effects of Intellectual property theft make clear the need to protect intellectual property. First, to the extent that piracy diminishes incentives to create new forms of intellectual property, fewer new products will be created, and businesses and consumers will enjoy fewer options in the marketplace. Second, intellectual property theft hits the Nation's most innovative economic sectors the hardest, and it is those sectors that are increasingly responsible for ensuring America's continuing prosperity and competitiveness. Third, theft of intellectual property can threaten public health and safety by introducing dangerous counterfeit products into the marketplace. Finally, the sizeable profits that can be generated at relatively low risk through intellectual property theft can invite additional criminal activity.

The economic impact of intellectual property theft is enormous. According to the Office of the United States Trade Representative ("USTR"), intellectual property theft costs American corporations $250 billion every year. Among those affected are manufacturers, distributors, retailers, employees, artists, consumers, and governments. These crimes also harm the economy through lost profits, taxes, and wages, and the loss of hundreds of thousands of jobs.

The costs of intellectual property theft are not solely economic. Intellectual property theft also affects the public's health and safety in costly ways. For instance, intellectual propertythieves can make enormous profits from selling cheap counterfeit versions of products whose safety and reliability are essential–including pharmaceuticals, automotive parts, and electrical equipment.

According to Business Week, counterfeit airplane parts played also affects the public's health and safety in cost a role in at least 166 U.S.-based accidents or mishaps during ly ways. For instance, intellectual property a recent 20-year period.

In addition to serious consequences for the economy and public health and safety, intellectual property theft is a concern because it can fund other criminal activities. Modern technology has increased the innovativeness of companies and the amount of new intellectual property being created, but it has also made intellectual property theft easier and more anonymous. Computer technology and the Internet generate inexpensive and far-flung opportunities for piracy and distribution. Such ease and profitability attract organized criminal enterprises to these offenses, and some of those enterprises may even have ties to terrorist organizations.

The United States Customs and Border Protection estimates that 750,000 American jobs have been lost due to counterfeiting.

Because of the serious consequences of intellectual property theft, combating these crimes is an important priority of the Department of Justice. In order to ensure a vibrant, innovative, and safe marketplace for all, the Department of Justice will continue to prosecute individuals and organizations that criminally infringe on intellectual property rights and vigorously protect the right of victims to pursue intellectual property cases in civil courts.

> *"Our ability to promote and secure an effective and predictable environment for intellectual property rights in America will have a significant impact on our future economic growth, global competitiveness, and economic national security."*
>
> - Attorney General Alberto R. Gonzales, November 10, 2005

Attorney General Alberto R. Gonzales addresses victims of intellectual property theft at the U.S. Chamber of Commerce's Anti-Counterfeiting and Piracy Summit. Photo by Ian Wagreich.

In: DOJ Progress Report on Intellectual Property ISBN: 978-1-60741-001-0
Editor: Todd B. Parker

Chapter 5

What Principles Should Apply to Intellectual Property Enforcement?

Department of Justice

The Department of Justice has developed a comprehensive, multi-dimensional strategy to fight intellectual property crime. This strategy addresses the many different, yet essential, aspects of intellectual property enforcement: criminal enforcement; international cooperation; civil and antitrust enforcement; and prevention. While the perspective and focus of each of these areas differ, they nonetheless are all united by underlying values that form the foundation of the Department of Justice's intellectual property efforts. The Task Force continues to adhere to these key principles that drive and shape the Department of Justice's intellectual property enforcement efforts, and provide a basis for recommending further actions. These principles are set forth below:

- **The laws protecting intellectual property rights must be enforced.** The Nation's economic security depends on the protection of valuable intellectual resources. The Department of Justice has a responsibility to enforce the criminal laws of the Nation that are designed to protect its economic security and the creativity and innovation of entrepreneurs.

- **The federal Government and intellectual property owners have a collective responsibility to take action against violations of federal intellectual property laws.**
  The federal Government has the primary responsibility for prosecuting violations of federal criminal laws involving intellectual property. The owners of intellectual property have the primary responsibility of protecting their creative works, marks, and trade secrets, and of pursuing civil enforcement actions.

- **The Department of Justice should take a leading role in the prosecution of the most serious violations of the laws protecting copyrights, marks, and trade secrets.**
  The Department of Justice has historically placed–and should continue to place–the highest priority on the prosecution of intellectual property crimes that are complex and large in scale, and that undermine our economic national security or threaten public health and welfare. The Department of Justice should continue to focus on these areas and enforce federal intellectual property laws as vigorously as resources will allow.

- **The federal Government should punish the misappropriation of innovative technologies rather than innovation itself.**
  The Department of Justice should enforce federal intellectual property laws in a manner that respects the rights of consumers, technological innovators, and content providers. The Department of Justice should prosecute those who misappropriate innovative technology or use technology to commit crimes, while ensuring that such enforcement efforts do not chill legitimate innovation.

- **Intellectual property enforcement must include the coordinated and cooperative efforts of foreign governments.**
  Violations of intellectual property laws are increasingly global in scope and involve offenders in many nations. Enforcement measures must therefore confront and deter foreign as well as domestic criminal enterprises. This requires the informal assistance of foreign governments and their law enforcement agencies, active enforcement of their own intellectual property laws, and formal international cooperation through treaties and international agreements.

In: DOJ Progress Report on Intellectual Property ISBN: 978-1-60741-001-0
Editor: Todd B. Parker

Chapter 6

How Has the Department of Justice Enforced and Protected Intellectual Property Rights?

Department of Justice

The Department of Justice comprehensively enforces and protects intellectual property rights through a number of divisions, sections, and agencies. Each of these important components has highly-trained attorneys, law enforcement agents, and staff who specifically address intellectual property issues, ranging from criminal prosecutions to antitrust concerns. In addition, the Bush Administration has developed a comprehensive, interagency initiative to combat intellectual property theft and address international enforcement issues. The Bush Administration's interagency campaigns and the Department of Justice's specific efforts are explained below.

A. Interagency Efforts – STOP Initiative and NIPLECC

The Department of Justice has the lead criminal enforcement role in the United States Government's protection of intellectual property rights here and abroad. The Department of Justice also coordinates with other government agencies on numerous domestic and international policy matters relating to intellectual property protection. It does so through a variety of means, including daily contact with other government agencies responsible for the many facets of intellectual property protection in the United States, as well as formal mechanisms such as the Bush Administration's Strategy Targeting Organized Piracy ("STOP") initiative and the National Intellectual Property Law Enforcement Coordination Council ("NIPLECC").

The Department of Justice has participated in the STOP initiative since its inception in 2004. STOP is a Bush Administration initiative that includes, among others, the Departments of Justice, Commerce, and Homeland Security, the Office of the United States Trade Representative, the USPTO, and the Food and Drug Administration. Through this initiative, the Bush Administration has sought to implement a government-wide plan to reduce counterfeiting and piracy throughout the world. The Department of Justice has made important contributions to this broad mission through the work of the Task Force and, more specifically, through implementation of the Task Force's detailed recommendations set forth in 2004 Report. The Department of Justice also has coordinated closely with other STOP agencies on numerous international and domestic policy issues; joined STOP agencies in visits to the European Commission, France, Germany, Hong Kong, Korea, and the United Kingdom in April and June of 2005; participated in a series of round table discussions, seminars, and other business outreach efforts; and helped develop greater public awareness of how federal criminal laws protect the owners of intellectual property.

> *"The Administration is leading an initiative called STOP–Strategy Targeting Organized Piracy. Nine federal agencies are coming together in this initiative, including the Department of Justice, which has launched the most aggressive effort in American history to prevent intellectual property violations."*
>
> \- President George W. Bush, March 16, 2006

The Department of Justice has also co-chaired NIPLECC since its creation by Congress in 1999. NIPLECC's mission is "to coordinate domestic and international intellectual property law enforcement among federal and foreign entities." Joining the Assistant Attorney General for the Criminal Division as co-chair of NIPLECC is the Under Secretary of Commerce for Intellectual Property and Director of the USPTO. Other NIPLECC members include the Under Secretary of State for Economic, Business, and Agricultural Affairs; a

Deputy United States Trade Representative; the Commissioner of Customs; the Under Secretary of Commerce for International Trade; and, in a consulting capacity, a representative from the United States Copyright Office. In July 2005, President Bush named Commerce Department official Chris Israel to the newly-created post of Coordinator of International Intellectual Property Enforcement, with responsibility for coordinating NIPLECC activities. Arif Alikhan, Senior Counsel to the Deputy Attorney General at the Department of Justice, serves as Deputy Coordinator. Together, Israel and Alikhan coordinate NIPLECC's international work and the overall implementation of the Bush Administration's STOP initiative.

NIPLECC helps ensure that the Bush Administration's intellectual property priorities are clear to Congress and the American public. In its annual report to Congress, NIPLECC describes the activities and actions taken by all NIPLECC members to improve the protection of intellectual property rights. NIPLECC also details the Department of Justice's enforcement strategy and priorities and highlights many of its most significant intellectual property prosecutions for that year. In addition, the Department of Justice works through NIPLECC to coordinate its international training and outreach efforts with other federal agencies.

President George W. Bush speaks about the STOP Initiative and the importance of protecting intellectual property during ceremonies at the Eisenhower Executive Office Building, March 16, 2006. Looking on are, from the left: Attorney General Alberto R. Gonzales; U.S. Rep. Jim Sensenbrenner (R-Wis); and U.S. Rep. Bobby Scott (D-Va.). Photo by Arif Alikhan.

B. Criminal Enforcement Efforts

1. Computer Crime and Intellectual Property Section

The Department of Justice has developed an effective nationwide anti-piracy and anti-counterfeiting effort anchored by the Criminal Division's Computer Crime and Intellectual Property Section ("CCIPS"). CCIPS is a highly specialized team of 35 attorneys focused on computer crime and intellectual property offenses. With the support of Congress, CCIPS has nearly doubled in size over the past six years, and it now has 14 attorneys devoted exclusively to prosecuting intellectual property crimes and implementing the Department of Justice's intellectual property enforcement program. These attorneys prosecute intellectual property cases, assist prosecutors in the field, and help develop and implement the Department of Justice's overall anti-piracy strategy and legislative priorities. In addition to prosecuting their own cases, which have increased more than eight-fold in the last four years, CCIPS attorneys are available to agents and Assistant United States Attorneys ("AUSAs") on a 24-hour basis to provide advice and guidance.

CCIPS also places a high priority on fostering international cooperation and coordination in its intellectual property enforcement efforts. Building relationships between American law enforcement and our counterparts overseas is the most effective method of ensuring success in multi-national cases. These relationships are built through international casework as well as through training and outreach. Last year, CCIPS attorneys met with more than 2,000 prosecutors, investigators, judges, and intellectual property experts from 94 countries to provide training and technical assistance on intellectual property enforcement.

2. Computer Hacking and Intellectual Property Program

As with all federal crime, primary responsibility for the prosecution of federal intellectual property offenses falls to the 94 United States Attorneys' Offices across America. Under the CHIP Program, created by then- Attorney General Ashcroft in 2001, experienced and highly-trained federal prosecutors in the field aggressively address computer crime and intellectual property matters.

a. CHIP Coordinators

Prior to the creation of the CHIP Program, in 1995 the Department of Justice created the Computer & Telecommunications Coordinator ("CTC") program to address concerns about the rising tide of computer crime. The United States Attorneys' Offices designated at least one AUSA in each district as a CTC; depending on the needs of the particular region, some districts designated more than one prosecutor. In addition, a number of components and divisions within the Department of Justice, such as the Tax Division, also designated CTCs for their respective organizations.

> *"The CHIP Program is a vital part of the & Telecommunications Coordinator ("CTC") pro Department of Justice's efforts to address the growgram to address concerns about the rising tide of com ing threat of cyber crime and intellectual property puter crime. The United States Attorneys' Offices des theft."*
>
> -Attorney General Alberto R. Gonzales, December 2, 2005

In October 2004, the Task Force recommended that the Department of Justice change the CTC designation to "CHIP Coordinator" to clarify that intellectual property offenses were included within the responsibilities of these AUSAs and to align all 94 United States Attorneys' Offices with the Attorney General's CHIP Program. Identifying a CHIP Coordinator in each United States Attorney's Office ensures that a prosecutor with training and experience in intellectual property crimes is available wherever and whenever an offense occurs.

Under the CHIP Program, prosecutors are assigned four areas of responsibility: (1) prosecuting computer crime and intellectual property offenses; (2) serving as a technical advisor for other prosecutors and law enforcement agents; (3) assisting other CHIP Coordinators in multi-district investigations; and (4) providing training and community outreach regarding computer-related issues.

b. CHIP Units

In July 2001, the Department of Justice created ten CHIP Units to address the increasing threat of cyber crime and intellectual property offenses in specific regions of the country. CHIP Units are teams of specially-trained AUSAs concentrated in a particular region. The CHIP Program was created to augment the number of prosecutors designated as CHIP Coordinators. The Department of Justice provided districts with additional funding to prosecutors and support personnel to form CHIP Units and to focus on fighting intellectual property and cyber offenses. The program was expanded in 2002 and 2004, including the effort in 2004 to align the CTC program with the CHIP Program described above. There are currently more than 230 CHIP Coordinators and CHIP Unit AUSAs within the Department of Justice.

CHIP Unit AUSAs focus on prosecuting intellectual property offenses such as trademark violations, copyright infringement, and thefts of trade secrets. They prosecute high-technology offenses, including hacking, virus and worm proliferation, Internet fraud, and other attacks on computer systems.

In addition to prosecuting cases, CHIP Unit AUSAs are also involved actively in training other prosecutors and federal agents on high-tech investigations, and they work closely with potential victims of intellectual property theft and cyber crime on prevention efforts.

The first CHIP Unit was created in February 2000, in the United States Attorney's Office in San Jose, California, to address cyber crime and intellectual property cases in the Silicon Valley area. Based on the success of the CHIP Unit in San Jose, in 2001 and 2002, then-Attorney General Ashcroft expanded the program to include the following 11 additional cities:

- Alexandria, Virginia
- Atlanta, Georgia
- Boston, Massachusetts
- Chicago, Illinois
- Dallas, Texas
- Kansas City, Missouri
- Los Angeles, California
- Miami, Florida
- New York, New York (Brooklyn and Manhattan)
- San Diego, California
- Seattle, Washington

In October 2004, the Task Force recommended that the Department of Justice create five more CHIP Units in:

- Nashville, Tennessee
- Orlando, Florida
- Pittsburgh, Pennsylvania
- Sacramento, California
- Washington, D.C.

In response, the Department of Justice subsequently provided additional funding to the United States Attorneys' Offices in these cities to hire additional prosecutors to create the CHIP Units.

In January 2005, the Department of Justice provided additional, full-time funding for three AUSAs to serve as CHIP Unit AUSAs in San Jose and Los Angeles, California. The creation of these three additional CHIP positions, as well as the creation of five additional CHIP Units in October 2004, implemented two of the recommendations of the 2004 Report.

c. Additional Accomplishment – Creation of Seven New CHIP Units in 2006

The Task Force has recognized the success of the CHIP Program and determined that the Department of Justice should increase the number of CHIP Units and place them in additional regions. Accordingly, the Task Force recommended to the Attorney General that the Department of Justice create seven new CHIP Units in the following cities where cyber crime and intellectual property offenses are significant problems:

- Austin, Texas
- Baltimore, Maryland
- Denver, Colorado
- Detroit, Michigan
- Newark, New Jersey
- New Haven, Connecticut
- Philadelphia, Pennsylvania

The Attorney General has adopted this recommendation and initiated the creation of these seven new units. With the addition of these new CHIP Units the total number of CHIP Units will soon be 25.

3. Office of Consumer Litigation

The Civil Division's Office of Consumer Litigation ("OCL") is a team of specialized attorneys who handle criminal and civil cases involving intellectual property laws that protect public health and safety. For example, OCL attorneys enforce and defend the consumer protection programs of the Food and Drug Administration ("FDA"), the Federal Trade Commission, the

Consumer Product Safety Commission, and the Department of Transportation's National Highway Traffic Safety Administration.

One particular area of concern to the protection of intellectual property rights and consumer safety is the regulation of drugs by the FDA. FDA officials have testified before Congress that the quality of drugs in this country is high and that the public can continue to have confidence that the drugs sold in the United States are authentic. To maintain this level of confidence, however, any allegations or information regarding the counterfeiting or adulteration of drug products must be taken very seriously. The use of counterfeit drugs can pose a direct threat to human health. Counterfeit drugs frequently contain less active material ingredient than claimed, wrong ingredients, or no active ingredient at all, which makes them less effective and possibly toxic. Even when the product in question contains the represented amount of the drug's active ingredient, the situation can be dangerous because of factors such as quality control, distribution, and inventory control, all of which endanger the effectiveness of the drug. When the counterfeit product is relied upon to sustain life, a lack of effectiveness may result in deaths. In addition, increased drug resistance also can arise when counterfeit antibiotics lead doctors to increase dosages or otherwise misunderstand the nature of the drug they are administering. The potential dangers posed by counterfeit drugs may multiply in a health emergency; for example, in a flu pandemic, the opportunity for criminal counterfeiting may be significant. The demand for flu vaccine could vastly exceed legitimate supply and counterfeit flu vaccine could be sold over the Internet to unwary consumers in the United States.

"The World Health Organization estimates that 10% of all available pharmaceuticals worldwide are counterfeit."

For more than 30 years, OCL attorneys have been involved in prosecuting purveyors of counterfeit drugs and medical devices. The Department of Justice's recent efforts are reflected in prosecutions involving unlawful diversion of prescription drugs and the importation of counterfeit pharmaceuticals and drugs that are not manufactured according to approved standards. United States Attorneys' Offices that receive these counterfeit cases often contact OCL to obtain advice and assistance, and OCL serves valuable functions in such matters. First, OCL helps ensure that federal prosecutors do not overlook important policy or factual concerns that frequently affect litigation under federal statutes. Second, OCL ensures that those prosecutors do not have to "reinvent the wheel" in conducting litigation, because OCL has jury instructions, briefs, and other pleadings to share.

4. Federal Law Enforcement Agencies

A number of federal law enforcement agencies work to safeguard intellectual property rights in the United States. The Federal Bureau of Investigation's ("FBI") intellectual property enforcement program is implemented and overseen by the Cyber Crime Fraud Unit ("FBI-CCFU") in its Cyber Division in Washington, D.C. The FBI-CCFU focuses on intellectual property crimes having the most impact on national and economic security–including theft of trade secrets, Internet piracy, and trafficking in counterfeit goods. The FBICCFU's goals include:

- Increasing the number of intellectual property undercover operations and use of other sophisticated investigative techniques;
- Developing new investigations through relationships with industry contacts and foreign law enforcement agencies;
- Encouraging FBI field offices to utilize task forces with state and local law enforcement agencies to enhance cyber crime and intellectual property investigations; and
- Continuing to educate and train domestic and foreign law enforcement agencies on intellectual property enforcement.

In addition to overseeing implementation of the intellectual property program in the 56 FBI field offices nationwide, the FBI-CCFU also plays a central and coordinating role in intellectual property undercover operations that have multi-district and international targets. In these operations, FBI-CCFU provides administrative oversight and additional resources to ensure the coordination of international and domestic enforcement actions. Examples of such enforcement initiatives were Operations Fast Link and Site Down, referenced below. The FBI-CCFU also provides guidance and assistance to field agents and foreign legal attachés' offices on intellectual property investigations generally, especially those targeting organized groups engaged in the large-scale manufacture and distribution of pirated software and other copyrighted materials over the Internet.

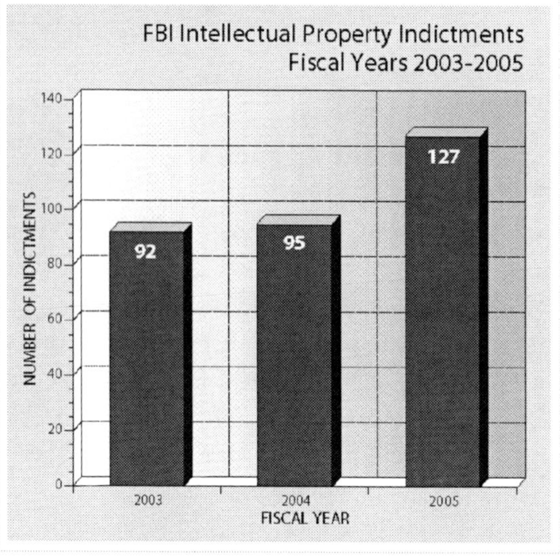

FBI Intellectual Property Indictments Fiscal Years 2003-2005

The FBI's intellectual property enforcement program has resulted in more investigations and more indictments in recent years. For instance, between Fiscal Year 2003 and Fiscal Year 2005, the number of open intellectual property investigations increased 22 percent, from 304 to 372 investigations per year, while the number of undercover investigations increased 87 percent. In addition, during the same time period, the number of indictments filed from intellectual property investigations increased 38 percent, from 92 to 127.

Apart from the FBI, other government agencies have jurisdiction to investigate certain intellectual property offenses, including the Department of Homeland Security's United States Immigration and Customs Enforcement ("ICE") and United States Customs and Border Protection ("CBP"). ICE and CBP, in conjunction with the National Intellectual Property Rights Coordination Center, work to identify and address growing intellectual property rights issues and criminal trends, particularly in shipments through ports of entry into the United States. ICE distributes that information to federal and state law enforcement through outreach and training as well as to foreign government and international law enforcement officials and prosecutors. Over the past few years, ICE investigators have seen an increase in the level of sophistication associated with the laundering and movement of money derived from the sale of counterfeit merchandise. In direct response to this growing problem, since 2001, ICE and CBP have initiated more than 31,000 seizures of counterfeit products with an estimated retail value in excess of $482 million. In addition, during that same five-year period, ICE has initiated more than 870 arrests for trafficking in counterfeit goods and related crimes that resulted in more than 455 federal criminal indictments and more than 495 convictions.

Finally, in addition to the FBI, ICE, and CBP, a number of other federal agencies investigate intellectual property offenses, whether on their own or as part of task forces, including the United States Postal Service and the United States Secret Service. The FDA's Office of Criminal Investigations has primary responsibility for all criminal investigations conducted by the FDA, which include investigations of suspected tampering incidents and suspected counterfeit products. For instance, its agents investigate cases involving counterfeit, misbranded, and adulterated pharmaceuticals in violation of federal drug laws.

5. Victim-Industry Partnerships

The Department of Justice recognizes that a successful and comprehensive plan of attack against intellectual property theft requires the formation of partnerships with the victims and potential victims of intellectual property theft. Without the assistance of victims, it is difficult, if not impossible, for the Department of Justice to enforce the law and apprehend offenders. Consequently, the Department of Justice has formed important partnerships with various organizations that have joined the fight against intellectual property theft. The Chamber of Commerce has formed a broad-based "Coalition Against Counterfeiting and Piracy" ("CACP"), which works with Congress and the Bush Administration to raise awareness about the negative impact of counterfeiting. The Department of Justice has formed a constructive partnership with the CACP to address intellectual property concerns and sponsor awareness events.

USED WITH PERMISSION OF THE
U.S. CHAMBER OF COMMERCE

"Without the assistance of victims, it is difficult, if not impossible, for the Department of Justice to enforce the law and apprehend offenders."

- Intellectual Property Task Force Vice Chairman Arif Alikhan,

April 27, 2006

The Department of Justice has also formed important partnerships with other groups that represent victims and potential victims of intellectual property theft, including the Motion Picture Association, the Recording Industry Association of America, the Business Software Alliance, the Electronic Software Association, pharmaceutical industry associations, and many other organizations. In addition, the Department of Justice has formed a close partnership with Court TV, which has filmed and broadcast several Department of Justice events regarding intellectual property. These organizations provide important insight into the problems of intellectual property theft and have joined the Department of Justice in sponsoring prevention and awareness events throughout the Nation

To assist these victims and others in reporting intellectual property crimes, the Department of Justice developed "A Guide for Victims of Counterfeiting, Copyright Infringement, and Theft of Trade Secrets," which is set forth in *Appendix B*.

6. Statistical Accomplishments

The impact of the increased efforts by the Department of Justice to protect intellectual property rights can be seen not only by the breadth of its programs and by the aggressive focus on this issue, but also by the impressive results in Department of Justice prosecutions. The Department of Justice has prosecuted significantly more defendants for intellectual property offenses since the issuance of the Task Force's Report in October 2004. During Fiscal Year 2005, 350 defendants were charged with intellectual property offenses, nearly double the 177 defendants charged in Fiscal Year 2004–representing a 98 percent increase. A similar increase occurred in districts with CHIP Units, where the number of charged defendants climbed from 109 in Fiscal Year 2004 to 180 in Fiscal Year 2005–a 65 percent increase. In addition, the number of cases filed and defendants charged in all districts between Fiscal Years 2001 and 2005 has steadily risen over time, as depicted in the accompanying graph on the following page. These results reflect, in a meaningful way, that the Department of Justice is committed to protecting intellectual property rights.

7. Intellectual Property Prosecution Highlights

As the preceding statistical analysis demonstrates, the Department of Justice has brought many significant prosecutions against intellectual property thieves since the Task Force issued its report in October 2004. The cases include prosecutions of defendants trafficking in counterfeit pharmaceuticals, of unauthorized distribution of copyrighted material, and of violations of the federal trademark laws. Some of the more notable cases include:

These graphs include data on any and all criminal cases/defendants where the following charges were brought as any charge against a defendant: 17 U.S.C. 1201 to 1205 (circumvention of copyright protection systems); 18 U.S.C. 1831 (economic espionage); 18 U.S.C. 1832 (theft of trade secrets); 18 U.S.C. 2318 (counterfeit labeling); 18 U.S.C. 2319 (criminal copyright infringement); 18 U.S.C. 2319A (live musical performance infringement); 18 U.S.C. 2320 (trafficking in counterfeit goods); or 47 U.S.C. 553 and 605 (signal piracy). However, the statutes were run together to eliminate any double counting of cases/defendants where more than one of the statutes was charged against the same defendant. This chart may not include criminal cases/defendants involving these offenses where the charges filed included only a conspiracy to violate any of the identified offenses. In addition, the data does not include month of September 2005 information for the Eastern District of Louisiana due to Hurricane Katrina.

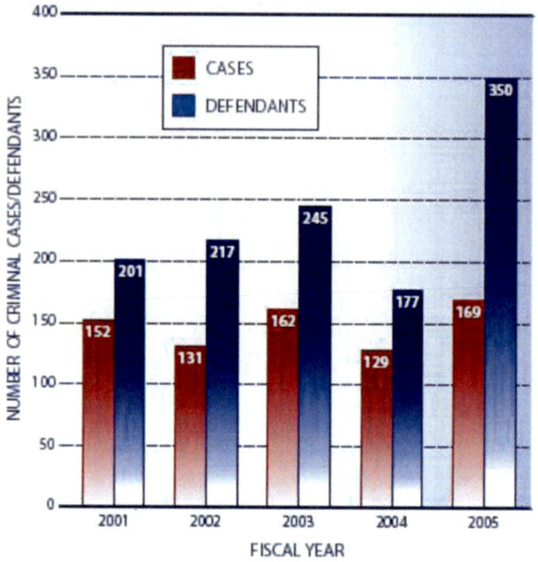

Source: Executive Office for United States Attorneys

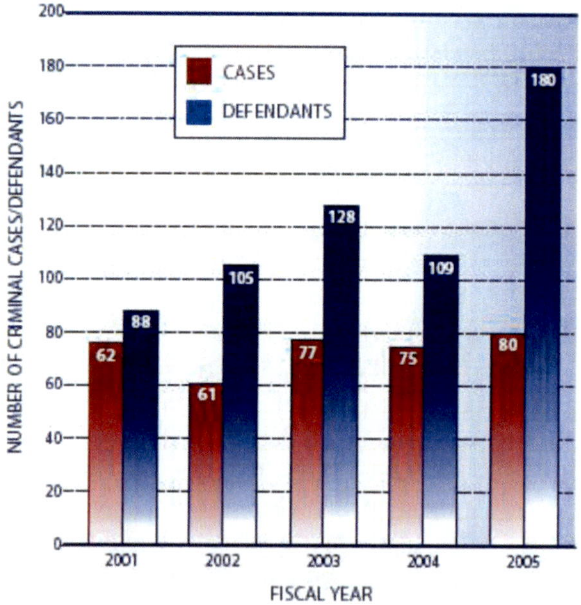

Source: Executive Office for United States Attorneys

Districts with Computer Hacking and Intellectual Property Units ("CHIP" Units)

Counterfeit Pharmaceuticals

Cholesterol Medication – The Department of Justice obtained convictions against eight people for selling counterfeit Lipitor tablets, a drug widely used to reduce cholesterol, and 13 people are awaiting trial in Kansas City, Missouri, for their alleged participation in a $42 million conspiracy to sell counterfeit, illegally imported, and misbranded Lipitor and other drugs. More than $2.2 million has been forfeited.

Antibiotics – In May 2005, the Department of Justice obtained the conviction of a former president of an Italian drug firm for violating the Federal Food, Drug, and Cosmetic Act by introducing an unapproved copy of the antibiotic Cefaclor. The defendant was sentenced to a year in confinement, fined $16,481,000, and required to forfeit $300,000. The corporate defendant pleaded guilty and paid criminal and civil penalties of more than $33 million.

The Center for Medicines in the Public Interest projects that counterfeit pharmaceutical revenues could grow from $35 billion in 2004 to $75 billion worldwide by 2010.

Viagra and Cialis – In February 2006, the Department of Justice obtained a conviction in Houston against a United States citizen for importing from China counterfeit pharmaceuticals bearing the Viagra and Cialis trademarks. ICE Special Agents conducted an undercover operation in Beijing, China, involving the Internet site bestonlineviagra.com. The Internet site was owned and used by the defendant to distribute bulk quantities of counterfeit Viagra and Cialis manufactured in China. Chinese officials cooperated in the investigation, and 11 additional individuals in China were arrested by Chinese authorities for manufacturing and distributing counterfeit drugs. Chinese officials seized 600,000 counterfeit Viagra labels and packaging, 440,000 counterfeit Viagra and Cialis tablets, and 260 kilograms of raw materials used to manufacture counterfeit pharmaceuticals.

> *"Our message to criminals who seek to profit from the intellectual property of honest and hard-working American citizens and businesses is clear: There is nothing fake about our commitment to prosecute counterfeiters and pirates."*
>
> \- Attorney General Alberto R. Gonzales, November 10, 2005

Viagra – In January 2005, the Department of Justice obtained the conviction of a Los Angeles man for manufacturing, importing, and distributing over 700,000 counterfeit Viagra tablets, valued at more than $5.5 million, over a four-year period.

Terrorism and Organized Crime

Terrorist Financing – In March 2006, a federal indictment was unsealed in Detroit charging 19 individuals with operating a racketeering enterprise that supported the terrorist organization Hizballah. The defendants are alleged to have financed their criminal enterprise by trafficking in counterfeit Viagra, by trafficking in counterfeit Zig-Zag papers and contraband cigarettes, and by producing counterfeit cigarette tax stamps.

Organized Crime – Yi Ging Organization – In April 2006, the Department of Justice obtained convictions against two Chinese nationals as part of a crackdown against a violent criminal group in New York known as the Yi Ging Organization. These defendants had been included, along with 39 others, in a September 2005 indictment charging racketeering offenses, including extortion, witness tampering, trafficking in counterfeit DVDs and CDs, money laundering, operating a large-scale illegal gambling business, and drug trafficking. The Yi Ging Organization allegedly generated millions of dollars in profits from their counterfeit DVD and CD business. Gang members traveled to China to obtain illegal copies of American and Chinese DVDs, which they then smuggled into the United States, copied, and sold along with pirated music CDs at stores the gang controlled in Manhattan and other parts of New York City.

Organized Crime – Operation Smoking Dragon – In Los Angeles, the Department of Justice obtained indictments against 30 defendants in August 2005 for allegedly, among other things, trafficking in counterfeit cigarettes and pharmaceuticals as part of Operation Smoking Dragon.

Software, Movie, and Music Piracy

International Enforcement Operations – The Department of Justice led the largest ever international enforcement efforts against organized online piracy in Operation FastLink and Operation Site Down. Each of these undercover operations by the FBI, involved coordinated law enforcement action among 12 countries and targeted elite, criminal organizations, known as "warez release groups," which are the first to provide pirated works on the Internet. Law enforcement agents conducted more than 200 searches and arrested numerous people worldwide, seized hundreds of thousands of pirated works conservatively valued at more than $100 million, and eliminated more than 20 major online distribution centers. To date, the Department of Justice has obtained convictions against 60 people in the United States on criminal copyright infringement charges.

> *"We will not be stopped by international borders in our vigorous pursuit of the technological pirates who steal products and profits from hard-working Americans."*
>
> - Assistant Attorney General for the Criminal Division, Alice S. Fisher, October 25, 2005

Illegal Manufacturing of DVDs in China – In the first joint criminal intellectual property investigation by the United States and China, known as Operation Spring, the Department of Justice obtained a conviction against the ringleader in a conspiracy to import 2,000 counterfeit DVDs of motion pictures. The defendant was convicted in China, along with three other co-conspirators, for selling more than 133,000 pirated DVDs to customers in more than 20 countries. After returning to the United States, the defendant was convicted again in Mississippi, sentenced to 45 months in prison, and ordered to forfeit more than $800,000.

Optical Disc Piracy – Operation Remaster – On April 3, 2006, the Department of Justice obtained convictions against two California men who pleaded guilty to conspiracy to mass-produce pirated music and software CDs. The two men were among five arrested as part of an undercover investigation targeting large-scale suppliers of pirated music and software. Agents seized nearly half a million pirated CDs and 5,500 high-speed, high-quality stampers used to make bootleg products. The recording industry called Operation Remaster the largest music manufacturing piracy seizure in United States history.

Online Music Piracy – On May 19, 2006, the Department of Justice obtained sentences of up to 15 months for three members of pre-release music piracy groups. Two of the defendants belonged to the Internet piracy group Apocalypse Crew, also known as "APC," and the third to the group

Chromance, also known as "CHR." Both groups sought to acquire digital copies of songs and albums before their commercial release in the United States, which they would then prepare for distribution to secure computer servers throughout the world. The stolen songs were then distributed globally and, within hours, filtered down to peer-to-peer and other public file-sharing networks.

Peer-to-Peer Piracy – Operation Gridlock – In January 2005, the Department of Justice obtained the first-ever criminal convictions for piracy through peer-to-peer networks when two operators of Direct Connect distribution centers pleaded guilty in Washington, D.C., to charges of conspiracy to commit criminal copyright infringement. Four defendants were convicted as a result of this FBI undercover investigation, code-named Operation Gridlock.

Counterfeit Software – In December 2005, the Department of Justice obtained convictions against a California man in Alexandria, Virginia, for selling copies of copyrighted software through his website, www.ibackups.net, and through the United States mail. The man sold, at prices substantially below the suggested retail price, more than $25 million in software products that were manufactured by Adobe Systems Inc., Macromedia, Inc., Microsoft Corporation, Sonic Solutions, and Symantec Corporation. He is believed to be the most prolific online commercial distributor of pirated software ever convicted in the United States.

In 2004, the Business Software Alliance estimates that the United States lost over $6.5 billion due to software piracy.

First Federal Camcording Conviction – In June 2005, a jury convicted a former Hollywood, California, resident of eight federal criminal charges, including three counts of copyright infringement, related to his use of a video camcorder to covertly film the motion pictures "The Core," "8 Mile," and "Anger Management" at private screenings for the purpose of making money. The defendant fled from the custody of his attorney on the evening of his last scheduled trial in 2003 and remained a fugitive for 16 months until the United States Marshals Service apprehended him in Florida.

Movie Piracy – Operation Copycat – On April 6, 2006, the Department of Justice obtained charges against five individuals who were "first-providers" of stolen movies on the Internet. Operation Copycat, a San Jose-based FBI undercover investigation, was one of three investigations contributing to Operation Site Down. The Department of Justice has obtained charges against 36 individuals and convicted 28, including the first convictions under the newly enacted Family Entertainment and Copyright Act for camcording movies and distributing pre-release works on the Internet.

Trafficking in Pirated Movies – Operation Western Pirates – On November 23, 2005, two men were convicted by a Puerto Rico jury for copyright infringement and trafficking in pirated motion pictures. The convictions resulted from Operation Western Pirates, an FBI movie piracy investigation in which approximately 50,000 pirated motion pictures in DVD and VHS format were seized from more than 25 locations in western Puerto Rico, including 23 video rental stores and three laboratories where employees manufactured the pirated movies. Agents also seized more than $125,000 in currency and approximately 450 pieces of computer and other electronic equipment.

> *"By stealing the creative product of talented people, two men were this form of piracy deprives artists of the rewards they deserve. If left unchecked, such crime would drain incentive to create that enriches our lives."*
>
> - Deputy Attorney General Paul J. McNulty, February 28, 2006

Satellite Signal Theft

DMCA Prosecution – In June 2005, the Department of Justice obtained the conviction of a New York man who violated the Digital Millennium Copyright Act ("DMCA") and mail fraud statutes by reprogramming Smart Cards to steal satellite programming from DISH Network. DISH Network electronically "scrambles" its satellite transmissions to prevent unauthorized viewing of its programming and, in order to receive services, its customers must purchase or lease satellite equipment that include Smart Cards inserted into the satellite receiver. The defendant sold approximately $308,000 of reprogrammed Smart Cards to others across the United States.

Luxury Goods

Trafficking in Counterfeit Hard Goods – In November 2005, the Department of Justice obtained indictments against four Massachusetts residents for laundering money and trafficking in more than 30,000 counterfeit luxury handbags and wallets, as well as the materials needed to make the counterfeits, worth more than $1.4 million. The defendants were alleged to have used 13 self-storage units in Massachusetts as the home base for one of New England's largest counterfeit goods operations, and they allegedly sold the counterfeit wallets and handbags at flea markets and to smaller gatherings at approximately 230 "purse parties" throughout the state.

Trade Secrets

Ohio Theft of Trade Secrets: The Department of Justice obtained convictions against an executive of an Ohio hydraulic pump manufacturer and a subsidiary of a South African competitor who stole the Ohio company's trade secrets. While still an employee of the Ohio company, the executive secretly assisted the South African subsidiary company by sharing financial and other confidential information in order to assist the competitor in establishing United States operations. The executive held clandestine meetings with representatives of the competitor in South Africa and elsewhere, and gave them surreptitious and unauthorized tours of the victim company's manufacturing facility.

Kentucky Theft of Trade Secrets: In April 2006, the Department of Justice obtained a 48-month prison sentence against a Kentucky man for conspiring to steal and sell trade secrets belonging to Corning, Inc. The defendant, while a Corning employee, stole drawings of Corning's Thin Filter Translator Liquid Crystal Display ("LCD") glass and sold the drawings to a corporation based in Taiwan that intended to compete with Corning in the production of LCD glass.

C. Legislative Efforts

Since the Task Force issued its report in October 2004, the Department of Justice has worked diligently with the Congress to enact legislation to further protect intellectual property rights. The 2004 Report listed several principles regarding legislation and, in several instances, Congress adopted those principles in drafting legislation. In addition, the Department of Justice developed a legislative package that was sent by the Administration to the Congress to further enhance intellectual property enforcement and protection. Set forth below are the three new laws passed since October 2004, and details of the legislative package proposed by the Administration.

Intellectual Property Protection and Courts Amendments Act of 2004 (H.R. 3632)

The Department of Justice supported the passage of the Intellectual Property Protection and Courts Amendment Act (H.R. 3632), which advanced the goal, set forth in the 2004 Report, of thwarting the distribution of counterfeit products and authorizing the seizure of the materials and equipment used to make them. The legislation expanded a previous law, which prohibited trafficking in counterfeit labels for copyrighted works, to also prohibit the trafficking in genuine but unauthorized labels. In addition, the legislation allowed the government to seize the equipment used in producing the counterfeit and illicit labels. The Bush Administration supported the legislation and offered suggestions for its improvement. The President signed the legislation on December 23, 2004.

Family Entertainment and Copyright Act of 2005 (S. 167)

In 2005, Congress enacted the Family Entertainment and Copyright Act of 2005 (S. 167). This legislation amended the federal criminal code to prohibit the knowing or attempted use of a video camera, or other audio-visual recording device, to make or transmit a copy of a motion picture or other copyrighted audiovisual work from a performance of such work in a movie theater or similar venue without authorization. The law established a maximum sentence of three years in prison for a first offense. The legislation also required the court to order the forfeiture and destruction of all unauthorized copies of the motion picture and any equipment used to carry out the violation. With reasonable cause, the owner, lessee, or employee of a theater is authorized to detain, in a reasonable manner for a reasonable time, suspected violators for questioning or to contact law enforcement.

In addition, this legislation established criminal penalties for the act of willful copyright infringement through distribution of certain copyrighted works being prepared for commercial distribution–including movies, software, games, and music–by making them available on a computer network accessible to members of the public, if the person knew, or should have known, that the work was intended for commercial distribution. Finally, the legislation directed the United States Sentencing Commission to review and potentially amend its guidelines for intellectual property crimes.

This legislation, and the related amendments to the United States Sentencing Guidelines, furthered two key principles identified in the 2004 Report: (1) the passive sharing of copyrighted works for unlawful distribution should be treated as the distribution of those works and should, where appropriate, be subject to prosecution; and (2) copyright law should recognize the premium value of a copyrighted work before the work is released for sale to the general public. A copy of a copyrighted work is more valuable before it can be legitimately obtained by anyone else. In such situations, not only is the "pre-release" copy more valuable, but it can also permit the holder to distribute copies as early as–or before–the copyrighted work's legitimate owner. As a result, although pre-release copies of a copyrighted work may not have a quantifiable retail value, they can be the most valuable copies of all, and their distribution can severely damage the rights holder.

President George W. Bush signs H.R. 32, the Stop Counterfeiting in Manufactured Goods Act, during ceremonies March 1 6, 2006, in the Eisenhower Executive Office Building. Looking on are, from left: Secretary Carlos Gutierrez, Department of Commerce; Secretary Elaine Chao, Department of Labor; Attorney General Alberto R. Gonzales, Department of Justice; U.S. Rep. Jim Sensenbrenner (RWis.); U.S. Rep. Joe Knollenberg (R-Mich.), and U.S. Rep. Bobby Scott (D-Va.). White House photo by Kimberlee Hewitt.

The President signed the Family Entertainment and Copyright Act into law in April 2005. As a result, the United States Sentencing Commission amended the United States Sentencing Guidelines to provide for an added penalty in cases involving a pre-release copyrighted work. The Bush Administration supported the passage of this legislation and the Department of Justice provided technical assistance to the Congress and the United States Sentencing Commission.

Stop Counterfeiting in Manufactured Goods Act (H.R. 32)

Based on the principles set forth in the 2004 Report, the Stop Counterfeiting in Manufactured Goods Act (H.R. 32) modified the federal criminal law relating to the trafficking in counterfeit goods and services by prohibiting trafficking in labels, documents, or packaging that bear counterfeit marks intended for goods or services. The legislation also expanded the definition of "trafficking" to include distribution of counterfeits for a wider variety of commercial purposes than was covered previously. Moreover, the legislation criminalized the possession of counterfeits with intent to distribute, as well as the importation and exportation of counterfeit goods. Finally, the statute subjected to forfeiture any article that bears or consists of a counterfeit mark, and any property derived from proceeds or used in the commission of the violation. The legislation was signed into law by President Bush on March 16, 2006.

> *"I will sign a bill that protects the hard work of American innovators, strengthens the rule of law, and helps keep our families and consumers safe."*
> - President George W. Bush, March 16, 2006

Intellectual Property Protection Act

In addition to the three already-enacted legislative packages relating to intellectual property, the Department of Justice has developed draft legislation, known as the Intellectual Property Protection Act of 2005, to further the goals established in the 2004 Report. This proposed legislation is designed to advance three general objectives. First, it would toughen penalties for intellectual property crimes by:

- Strengthening of the repeat-offender penalties that are against copyright criminals;

- Implementing broad forfeiture reforms that, among other things, ensure the ability to seize and obtain forfeiture of property derived from or used in the commission of intellectual property offenses; and
- Strengthening a victim's ability to recover losses for certain intellectual property crimes (e.g., criminal copyright and Digital Millennium Copyright Act offenses).

"This legislative package, if enacted, would strengthen penalties for repeat copyright criminals, expand criminal intellectual property protection, and add critical investigative tools for both criminal and civil enforcement."
- Attorney General Alberto R. Gonzales, November 10, 2005

Second, the bill would expand the criminal laws to increase intellectual property protection by:

- Clarifying that registration of a copyright is not a prerequisite to criminal prosecution;
- Criminalizing the attempt to commit copyright infringement; and
- Clarifying that both the exportation and importation of infringing items is illegal, even if the export or import is not to a third party (*e.g.*, when the shipment is from one party to itself).

Third, the bill would add needed investigative tools for criminal and civil enforcement by:

- Amending civil copyright law to parallel civil trademark law by permitting civil litigants to obtain *ex parte* seizure orders for records or evidence in civil cases; and
- Amending 18 U.S.C. § 2516 to include, as predicate offenses necessary to obtain wire or oral intercepts, the crimes of economic espionage to benefit a foreign government, criminal copyright infringement, and trafficking in counterfeit goods or services.

The Intellectual Property Protection Act is an important legislative effort because it encourages the adoption of vital principles set forth in the 2004 Report, including the following:

- **As with other laws involving intellectual property, an attempt to violate the criminal copyright statute should be a violation without regard to whether it is successful.**
  Unlike the federal criminal trademark statute, the criminal copyright statute presently does not criminalize attempted violations. It is a general tenet of criminal law, however, that those who attempt to commit a crime are as morally culpable as those who succeed in doing so.

- **Law enforcement officers should have access to the full range of accepted law enforcement tools when they investigate intellectual property crimes that pose a serious threat to public health or safety.**
  A federal court may issue an order authorizing the use of a wire or voice intercept, otherwise known as a "wiretap," in the investigation of many federal crimes, including the theft of interstate shipments, but not for intellectual property crimes. Although there are good reasons to restrict the use of wiretaps in deference to individual privacy rights, some intellectual property crimes present a serious danger to public health or safety. Trademark violations, for instance, may involve the distribution of counterfeit goods that are defective and prone to causing widespread consumer injuries.

The Department of Justice's Task Force recommends that the Congress enact the Intellectual Property Protection Act at its earliest opportunity.

International Treaties

With the globalization of the economy and the rise of digital commerce, intellectual property crimes have crossed international borders with increasing frequency. To account for this trend, the United States has signed two treaties that currently are pending before the Senate: The United Nations Convention Against International Organized Crime, and the Council of Europe Convention on Cybercrime. These treaties would facilitate international cooperation in halting some of the most egregious crimes involving intellectual property. To further international cooperation and enforcement efforts, the Department of Justice supports the ratification of these treaties, but the Senate has not yet voted on them. The Task Force continues to recommend the expeditious ratification of both treaties.

D. Civil Enforcement Efforts – Civil Division

The Department of Justice combats intellectual property theft most visibly through enforcement of the Nation's criminal laws. The successful defense of intellectual property rights, however, also requires vigorous enforcement by the owners of intellectual property through the civil justice system.

The Department of Justice has filed numerous briefs, known as "*amicus*" or "friend-of-the-court" briefs, in the Supreme Court and lower courts supporting the maintenance and implementation of robust intellectual property rights. The Department of Justice also intervenes in appropriate cases to become a party in the litigation, thus promoting legal precedents that enforce intellectual property rights fairly and consistently. In these ways, the Department of Justice plays a vital role in promoting a legal environment that protects creativity and innovation. The Civil Division employs 14 lawyers devoted solely to intellectual property, as well as numerous appellate attorneys who assist with *amicus* filings as needed.

"The Department of Justice takes intellectual property issues seriously, and we are doing something about them, both criminally and civilly."
- Associate Attorney General Robert D. McCallum, Jr., March 2, 2006

Through these components, the Department of Justice also monitors civil enforcement developments that may hamper the ability of victims of intellectual property theft to use the civil courts effectively to defend themselves. For example, the Department of Justice actively consults with the USPTO and the United States Copyright Office about intellectual property cases. The Department of Justice also regularly reviews intellectual property trade publications, such as the Bureau of National Affairs' *Patent, Trademark, and Copyright Journal, and the United States Patents Quarterly's* advance sheets, to determine if any private lawsuits merit involvement by the Department of Justice.

Since October 2004, the Department of Justice has filed 13 *amicus* briefs in the Supreme Court in cases involving intellectual property rights, and more than a dozen *amicus* briefs and Statements of Interest in lower courts. These filings occurred in cases that affect numerous high-tech industries, including pharmaceuticals, biotechnology, and online commerce. In many of these cases, courts have adopted the arguments made by the Department of Justice and consequently expanded protections for owners of intellectual property rights.

Detailed explanations of these cases are set forth below in the Civil Recommendation section of this Progress Report.

E. ANTITRUST ENFORCEMENT EFFORTS – ANTITRUST DIVISION

The Antitrust Division of the Department of Justice, the component charged with enforcing the federal antitrust laws, does not directly enforce intellectual property rights. But intellectual property plays an increasingly important role in the Department of Justice's antitrust merger and non-merger civil investigations. Intellectual property is an asset that can be bought, sold, and leased or licensed in much the same fashion as any other property. The Department of Justice therefore applies antitrust principles that give the same respect to intellectual property as to other forms of tangible or intangible property, taking into account special characteristics of intellectual property, such as the ease with which it can be misappropriated. Using this approach, the Department of Justice avoids creating intellectual property-specific rules that could conflict with normal business expectations, lead to marketplace uncertainty, or erode the value of intellectual property rights over time.

> "*Our systems of effective antitrust enforcement and strong intellectual property rights protection complement each other—they each foster dynamic competition that generates lower prices, greater innovation, and wider choice, which makes consumers better off.*"
>
> - Assistant Attorney General for the Antitrust Division, Thomas O. Barnett, May 15, 2006

The Department of Justice promotes respect for intellectual property rights in the administration of antitrust law through international competition advocacy, as explained later in this Progress Report. Domestically, the Department of Justice engages in competition advocacy through public hearings, workshops, speeches, research, and academic publishing by its attorneys and economists (in the Antitrust Division's Economic Analysis Group), and through participation in court cases as *amicus curiae*.

Since the issuance of the 2004 Report, the United States has appeared as *amicus* in numerous antitrust cases involving intellectual property. The Supreme Court followed the recommendation of the United States in two such cases: *Illinois Tool Works, Inc. v. Independent Ink, Inc.*, 126 S. Ct. 1281

(2006), and *Monsanto Co. v. McFarling,* 125 S. Ct. 2956 (2005), which are described in more detail later in this Progress Report in the Civil Recommendation section.

The Department of Justice continues to participate as *amicus* in cases where the interplay of intellectual property and antitrust law presents an opportunity to strengthen or clarify intellectual property rights. In addition, the Department of Justice routinely reviews and comments on proposed legislation that involves issues at the intersection of antitrust and intellectual property, or that may influence incentives to engage in competition or innovation.

The Antitrust Division also provides trade associations and other business organizations a business review procedure to receive guidance from the Department of Justice regarding the scope, interpretation, and application of the antitrust laws to proposed conduct, including activities involving intellectual property rights. Under that procedure, persons concerned, for example, about whether a particular proposed standard-setting activity is legal under the antitrust laws may ask the Department of Justice for a statement of its current enforcement intentions with respect to that conduct. When sufficient information and documents are submitted to the Department of Justice, it will make its best effort to resolve the business review request within 60 to 90 days. In this way, the Department of Justice can protect competition while at the same time facilitating efficient business arrangements that enable intellectual property owners to protect their rights.

F. International Efforts — Free Trade Agreements

Since the 2004 Report was issued, the Department of Justice has worked closely with the United States Trade Representative ("USTR") on interagency development of trade policy issues affecting competition and intellectual property rights and on participation in negotiations concerning Free Trade Agreements ("FTAs") with foreign trading partners. The most recent negotiations concerned FTAs with Australia, South Korea, and Thailand. To enhance the Department of Justice's involvement in the process, Department of Justice attorneys in the Antitrust, Civil, and Criminal Divisions have undertaken a comprehensive review of existing FTAs and proposed a series of recommendations to USTR to strengthen support for intellectual property rights enforcement in the intellectual property rights chapters of FTAs and other trade pacts. After a series of discussions, USTR adopted several of the Department of Justice's recommendations, including: (1) revising language to ensure that foreign courts have the authority to order infringers to provide intellectual property owners with access to information relevant to an infringement; (2) adding language to ensure that FTA partners adopt policies or guidelines that encourage their courts to impose penalties, including sentences of actual imprisonment, at levels sufficient to constitute a deterrent to intellectual property theft; (3) expanding language to ensure that FTA partners provide for presumptions in civil, criminal, and administrative proceedings that intellectual property rights are valid and enforceable; (4) ensuring that foreign courts have the authority to order the infringer to pay the intellectual property rights holder's attorney's fees and other litigation costs; and (5) restricting the ability of FTA partners to order compulsory licensing of patents and clarifying that patents should not be presumed to create antitrust market power. The Department of Justice recognizes the importance of strengthening intellectual property rights through international agreements, and it will continue to work closely with USTR on an ongoing basis.

In: DOJ Progress Report on Intellectual Property ISBN: 978-1-60741-001-0
Editor: Todd B. Parker

Chapter 7

WHAT IS THE STATUS OF THE INTELLECTUAL PROPERTY TASK FORCE'S RECOMMENDATIONS?

Department of Justice

Immediately after the 2004 Report was released in October 2004, the Department of Justice began implementing the recommendations of the Task Force. For example, the Department of Justice immediately distributed the funding necessary to create five new CHIP Units and to supplement the prosecutors in the Central and Northern Districts of California. In addition, the Department of Justice began implementing many of the long-term recommendations, including drafting a package of legislative proposals consistent with the principles set forth in the 2004 Report.

In February 2005, Attorney General Alberto R. Gonzales renewed the Department of Justice's commitment to the Task Force by appointing new members. Importantly, he announced that the Department of Justice would implement all of the 2004 Report's recommendations and would continue to enforce aggressively federal intellectual property laws. As of this publication, the Department of Justice has implemented all 31 of the recommendations contained in the 2004 Report.

The Task Force formed an Executive Staff of experts from throughout the Department of Justice to implement the recommendations and draft this

Progress Report. The following sections set forth each of the recommendations and indicate their status as follows:

- IMPLEMENTED – the Department of Justice has fully implemented the recommendation.
- IMPLEMENTED AND ONGOING – the Department of Justice has implemented the recommendation, which requires an ongoing commitment and action.

A. Criminal Enforcement Recommendations

Enforcement of the criminal intellectual property laws is one of the Department of Justice's highest priorities. The Attorney General has stated on several occasions that criminal enforcement is an important and essential effort in the fight against intellectual property theft.

The Department of Justice prosecutes criminal cases involving the theft of copyrighted works, trademark counterfeiting, and thefts of trade secrets. Many divisions and offices of the Department of Justice participate in the enforcement of intellectual property laws, including federal prosecutors located throughout the Nation. These prosecutors work closely with local, State, and federal law enforcement agents to identify criminals and prosecute them in accordance with the law. While the Department of Justice has successfully prosecuted numerous intellectual property cases over the past several years, the Task Force concluded that additional success was possible. Accordingly, the Task Force made recommendations to further expand and strengthen the fight against intellectual property crime. Those recommendations and their status are set forth below.

(1) Create five additional Computer Hacking and Intellectual Property ("CHIP") Units in regions of the country where intellectual property producers significantly contribute to the national economy. These areas are the District of Columbia; Sacramento, California; Pittsburgh, Pennsylvania; Nashville, Tennessee; and Orlando, Florida;

STATUS: IMPLEMENTED

(2) Reinforce and expand existing CHIP Units located in key regions where intellectual property offenses have increased, and where the CHIP Units have effectively developed programs to prosecute CHIP-related cases, coordinate law enforcement activity, and promote public awareness programs;

STATUS: IMPLEMENTED

(3) Designate CHIP Coordinators in every federal prosecutors' office and make the coordinators responsible for intellectual property enforcement in that region;

STATUS: IMPLEMENTED

(4) Examine the need to increase resources for the Computer Crime and Intellectual Property Section of the Criminal Division in Washington, D.C., to address additional intellectual property concerns;

STATUS: IMPLEMENTED

(5) Recommend that the FBI increase the number of Special Agents assigned to intellectual property investigations, as the Department of Justice itself increases the number of prosecutors assigned to intellectual property enforcement concerns;

STATUS: IMPLEMENTED AND ONGOING

(6) Recommend that the FBI increase the number of personnel assigned to search for digital evidence in intellectual property cases;

STATUS: IMPLEMENTED AND ONGOING

(7) Dismantle and prosecute more nationwide and international criminal organizations that commit intellectual property crimes;

STATUS: IMPLEMENTED

(8) Enhance programs to train prosecutors and law enforcement agents investigating intellectual property offenses;

STATUS: IMPLEMENTED

(9) Prosecute aggressively intellectual property offenses that endanger the public's health or safety;

STATUS: IMPLEMENTED AND ONGOING

(10) Emphasize the importance of charging intellectual property offenses in every type of investigation where such charges are applicable, including organized crime, fraud, and illegal international smuggling;

STATUS: IMPLEMENTED AND ONGOING

(11) Enhance its program of educating and encouraging victims of intellectual property offenses and industry representatives to cooperate in criminal investigations. Recommended enhancements include:

(A) Encouraging victims to report intellectual property crime to law enforcement agencies;

STATUS: IMPLEMENTED AND ONGOING

(B) Distributing the new "Department of Justice Guide to Reporting Intellectual Property Crime" to victims and industry representatives regarding federal intellectual property offenses; and

STATUS: IMPLEMENTED AND ONGOING

(C) Hosting a conference with victims and industry representatives to educate participants on how they can assist in law enforcement investigations; and

STATUS: IMPLEMENTED

(12) Issue internal guidance to federal prosecutors regarding how victims can assist prosecutors in intellectual property cases.

Criminal Enforcement Recommendation #1

Expand The CHIP Program By Adding Five New Units

Recommendation: The Department of Justice should create five additional CHIP Units in regions of the country where intellectual property producers significantly contribute to the national economy. These areas are (1) the District of Columbia; (2) Sacramento, California; (3) Pittsburgh, Pennsylvania; (4) Nashville, Tennessee; and (5) Orlando, Florida.

STATUS: IMPLEMENTED

Explanation: In 2005, the Department of Justice funded five new CHIP Units in: the District of Columbia; Sacramento, California; Pittsburgh, Pennsylvania; Nashville, Tennessee; and Orlando, Florida. A total of ten new AUSA positions were allocated to these Units. This fully implemented the Task Force's recommendation.

CHIP prosecutors focus on copyright and trademark violations, theft of trade secrets, computer intrusions, theft of computer and high-tech components, and Internet fraud. In addition, CHIP Unit prosecutors develop public awareness programs and provide training to other prosecutors and law enforcement agencies regarding high-tech issues. During the 2003 fiscal year, the first full year after all 13 of the CHIP Units became operational, the offices with CHIP Units filed charges against 46 percent more defendants than they had averaged in the four fiscal years prior to the formation of the units. Similar improvement and results are forecast for the five new Units created in 2004.

Supplemental Recommendation For New Chip **Units:** Recognizing the success of the CHIP Unit program, the task force has recommended to the Attorney General the creation of additional CHIP Units in areas where intellectual property theft and cyber crime are significant problems. After reviewing submissions from various United States Attorneys' Offices and analyzing resource needs, The Department of Justice recently created seven new CHIP Units in the following cities:

- Austin, Texas
- Baltimore, Maryland
- Denver, Colorado

- Detroit, Michigan
- Newark, New Jersey
- New Haven, Connecticut
- Philadelphia, Pennsylvania

With the addition of these seven new Units, which are well above the number recommended by the Task Force in October 2004, the total number of CHIP Units nationally will be 25. To ensure consistency with the national CHIP Program, the Department of Justice has issued guidance to all United States Attorneys in districts with new and existing CHIP Units regarding expectations for the use of CHIP Program resources.

Criminal enforcement recommendation #2

Reinforce and Expand CHIP Units in Key Regions

Recommendation: The Department of Justice should reinforce and expand existing CHIP Units located in key regions where intellectual property offenses have increased, and where the CHIP Units have effectively developed programs to prosecute chip-related cases, coordinate law enforcement activity, and promote public awareness programs.

STATUS: IMPLEMENTED

Explanation: In January 2005, the attorney general provided additional, full-time funding for a total of three ausas to serve as chip prosecutors in the central and northern districts of california.

The Central and Northern regions of California historically have had especially heavy intellectual property caseloads. Los Angeles, for example, has approximately 18 million people, hosts the largest seaport in the world, and is home to a thriving entertainment industry, numerous high-tech businesses, and universities. San Jose is the center of the intellectual property-based economy of Silicon Valley. Both the San Jose and Los Angeles regions have a large economic base and numerous actual and potential victims of intellectual property theft. Moreover, the existing CHIP Units in these districts have been the most productive in the country in terms of intellectual property prosecutions. Accordingly, these districts were provided additional prosecutors to cope with the high incidence and severe regional impact of intellectual property crimes.

Criminal Enforcement Recommendation #3

Designate CHIP Coordinators in Every Federal Prosecutor's Office in the Nation

Recommendation: The Department of Justice should designate CHIP Coordinators in every federal prosecutor's office and make the coordinators responsible for intellectual property enforcement in that region.

STATUS: IMPLEMENTED

Explanation: In 1995, the Department of Justice created the Computer and Telecommunications ("CTC") Program, which designated at least one federal prosecutor to prosecute cyber crime within each district. CTCs were made responsible for providing technical advice to fellow prosecutors, assisting other CTCs in multi-district investigations, and coordinating public awareness efforts.

In October 2004, the Department of Justice re-designated all CTCs as CHIP Coordinators to better align all 94 United States Attorney's Offices with the Attorney General's CHIP Unit Program, announced in 2001, as well as the enforcement mission of CCIPS in Washington, D.C. The addition of "Intellectual Property" in the title helped clarify the CHIP Coordinator's responsibility to prosecute intellectual property offenses and coordinate public awareness and training efforts on intellectual property crime within the district.

The Department of Justice has increased overall CHIP attorney numbers by nearly 30 percent in the past four years to approximately 230 nationally, with at least one, and frequently more than one, CHIP Coordinator in every United States Attorney's Office. Moreover, the Department of Justice has issued guidance to all United States Attorneys clarifying the role of CHIP Coordinators in prosecuting both computer crime and intellectual property offenses.

Criminal Enforcement Recommendation #4

Examine The Need To Increase CCIPS Resources

Recommendation: The Department of Justice should examine the need to increase resources for the Computer Crime and Intellectual Property Section of the Criminal Division in Washington, D.C., to address additional intellectual property enforcement concerns.

STATUS: IMPLEMENTED

Explanation: The Department implemented this recommendation by formally seeking funding for two additional prosecutor positions in the Criminal Division's CCIPS for the 2007 budget year. The President has forwarded the request to Congress as part of the Bush Administration's Fiscal Year 2007 Budget submission.

The past four years have seen a marked evolution in the Criminal Division's intellectual property rights enforcement efforts. CCIPS has made the investigation and prosecution of large-scale, multinational intellectual property cases a top priority, and has increased its intellectual property caseload by nearly 800 percent, from 23 pending cases and investigative matters at the beginning of Fiscal Year 2002, to 203 cases and investigations at the beginning of Fiscal Year 2006. In addition to prosecuting cases, CCIPS develops Department of Justice programs and policies to address important aspects of intellectual property enforcement, and it provides legislative advice to lawmakers.

Currently, there are 14 prosecutors in CCIPS dedicated to the enforcement of intellectual property rights. In light of CCIPS's proactive prosecution strategy and its markedly increased workload, the Department of Justice recognized that CCIPS both needed and deserved additional resources. The Task Force recommends that the Congress fully fund the President's Fiscal Year 2007 request for additional prosecutors for CCIPS.

Criminal Enforcement Recommendation #5

Increase the Number of FBI Agents Assigned to Intellectual Property Investigations

Recommendation: The Department of Justice should recommend that the FBI increase the number of Special Agents assigned to intellectual property investigations, as the Department of Justice itself increases the number of prosecutors assigned to intellectual property enforcement.

STATUS: IMPLEMENTED AND ONGOING

Explanation: The FBI has proven its tremendous investigative and technical capabilities in numerous complex intellectual property cases prosecuted by the Department of Justice, including multi-district investigations and technically sophisticated enforcement actions. In addition, FBI agents are on the front line of criminal investigations, and they are typically the first responders when trade secret thefts or other intellectual property crimes are reported.

Since the 2004 Report was issued, the FBI has revised its Cyber National Strategy and made investigating intellectual property crimes a top priority of the Cyber Division. Moreover, the FBI has increased its domestic and international training programs for FBI Special Agents and task force members. For example, in February 2006, the FBI hosted a seminar for more than 100 FBI Special Agents on intellectual property investigations. The seminar included presentations from numerous victim-industry groups, such as representatives from the pharmaceutical, luxury goods, motion picture, software, and automotive manufacturing industries. The training included methods for investigation of intellectual property cases and legal instruction.

The FBI has increased the number of personnel assigned to investigating intellectual property violations by frequently assigning Supervisory Special Agents and Investigative Analysts from FBI Headquarters in Washington, D.C., to FBI field offices throughout the country. These specially-trained personnel have been temporarily deployed to major cities such as Atlanta, Georgia; Chicago, Illinois; Los Angeles and San Francisco, California; as well as smaller cities including Oklahoma City, Oklahoma and Richmond, Virginia. These agents and analysts provide significant guidance, analytical support, and investigative assistance in complex intellectual property matters.

Pictured at a press conference is Attorney General Alberto R. Gonzales and FBI Director Robert S. Mueller . Photo by Lonnie D. T ague.

The FBI also provides law enforcement training to numerous international partners on intellectual property issues. From January 2005 through May 2006, FBI Special Agents have traveled to Brazil, Cambodia, China, India, Iceland, Italy, and the United Kingdom to train law enforcement officers on intellectual property investigations. The FBI has also provided, in the United States, training to numerous international visitors in conjunction with the USPTO.

While the FBI has produced numerous cases with limited resources, it is constantly reviewing methods to increase the number of Special Agents assigned to intellectual property crime. Through increased training and the hard work of its Special Agents, the FBI has increased the number of indictments involving intellectual property offenses by 38 percent in Fiscal Year 2005, and it will continue to pursue aggressively investigations involving intellectual property offenses.

Criminal Enforcement Recommendation #6

Increase FBI Personnel Assigned to Search for Digital Evidence

Recommendation: The Department of Justice should recommend that the FBI increase the number of personnel assigned to search for digital evidence in intellectual property cases.

STATUS: IMPLEMENTED AND ONGOING

Explanation: Digital evidence is often the foundation of successful intellectual property prosecutions, particularly in online piracy investigations. The Department of Justice's ability to locate and interpret this evidence is therefore a critical factor in obtaining convictions and identifying other criminals. Information found on computers and other digital devices, such as cell phones and personal digital assistants, is also essential evidence in many intellectual property prosecutions. Timely computer forensic examinations are necessary to identify the offenders, analyze the stolen materials, and determine whether additional evidence is needed before criminal charges can be filed. Consequently, increasing the number of personnel who can examine digital evidence is critical to ensuring swift investigations and prosecutions.

To respond effectively to the increased sophistication of intellectual property theft, the FBI has increased the amount of FBI personnel available to review forensic evidence and to maintain its advantage over high-tech intellectual property criminals in the following three ways:

1. Case Agent Investigative Review ("CAIR") Program

Since the issuance of the 2004 Report, the FBI has increased its efforts to explore methods to streamline the computer forensic examination process. One method that the FBI has expanded to its 56 field offices is the CAIR program. Based on a pilot program in FBI Field Offices in Los Angeles and Washington, D.C., the FBI has trained approximately 1,000 Special Agents and other investigators to review evidence seized from computers. In addition to the case agents reviewing computer evidence, specially-trained Computer Analysis Response Team ("CART") forensic examiners analyze and examine computer evidence that is seized during the course of a criminal investigation. These highly- trained examiners assist the case agents in the CAIR process and also perform independent analyses and examinations.

2. CART Storage Area Network ("CARTSAN")

Another method for increasing the number of personnel equipped to review computer evidence is through the CARTSAN program. This program involves a network of computers that specially-trained FBI agents use to review–from their desktops–copies of seized computer evidence. There are 23 systems in the CARTSAN program, and 15 FBI field offices have the ability to share computer evidence with each other. CARTSAN speeds up the initial review of seized digital evidence and helps maximize the productive use of existing CART resources by allowing more FBI personnel to review the critical evidence that is often found on seized computers.

3. Regional Computer Forensic Laboratories ("RCFLs")

The FBI's third method to increase the number of personnel available to examine digital evidence is through the RCFL program. An RCFL is a regional lab for examining computer evidence seized during criminal investigations by various State, local, and federal law enforcement agencies. It is a full- service forensics laboratory and training center devoted to examining digital evidence in support of FBI criminal investigations–including investigations of theft of intellectual property, terrorism, child pornography, violent crimes, Internet crimes, and fraud.

RCFLs exist in the following cities:

- Chicago, Illinois
- Dallas, Texas
- Denver, Colorado
- Hamilton, New Jersey
- Houston, Texas
- Kansas City, Missouri
- Menlo Park, California
- Portland, Oregon
- Salt Lake City, Utah
- San Diego, California

Four additional RCFLs are scheduled to open by the end of 2006 in Buffalo, New York; Dayton, Ohio; Louisville, Kentucky; and Philadelphia, Pennsylvania. This will bring the total number of RCFLs to 14.

Criminal Enforcement Recommendation #7

Target Large, Complex Criminal Organizations That Commit Intellectual Property Crimes

Recommendation: The Department of Justice should dismantle and prosecute more nationwide and international criminal organizations that commit intellectual property crimes.

STATUS: IMPLEMENTED

Explanation: Since the inception of the Task Force in April 2004, the Department of Justice has led the two largest international enforcement efforts ever undertaken against organized online piracy. Operations FastLink and Site Down each involved coordinated law enforcement action among 12 countries and attacked the highest levels of the criminal groups–known as "warez release groups"–that act as first-providers of pirated software, movies, games, and music to the Internet. Together, these operations resulted in approximately 210 searches or arrests worldwide; the seizure of hundreds of thousands of pirated works conservatively valued at more than $100 million; the elimination of more than 20 major online distribution centers; and, to date, convictions of 60 individuals on criminal copyright infringement charges.

The Department of Justice's enforcement efforts against organized criminal groups have not been limited to online piracy. In the past two years, the Department of Justice has conducted a number of investigations and prosecutions of organized crime groups that traffic in counterfeit manufactured goods.

For instance, in November 2004, federal agents in New York arrested 28 individuals who were members of criminal organizations allegedly engaged in attempted murder, loan sharking, alien smuggling, narcotics distribution, gambling, and trafficking in counterfeit clothing accessories. The arrests included members of two Asian criminal enterprises operating in Manhattan's Chinatown and in Flushing, Queens. Twelve of the gangs' members were charged federally with criminal racketeering, and 24 individuals connected with the criminal enterprises have since pleaded guilty to numerous federal charges. These criminal organizations' illegal activities included selling counterfeit Chanel, Gucci, and Coach accessories at stores they owned in Midtown Manhattan, as well as distributing the counterfeit apparel to other retail outlets.

As reflected in these cases and others, organized crime in intellectual property theft and counterfeiting cases is a global enforcement problem. In the past two years, the Department of Justice has successfully dismantled and prosecuted more of these criminal groups than ever before. The increase in such prosecutions is reflected in case statistics from Fiscal Year 2003 through Fiscal Year 2005, which show a general rise in the number of defendants being charged per case. In Fiscal Year 2003, 245 defendants were charged in 162 cases, for an average of 1.51 defendants per case; in Fiscal Year 2004, 177 defendants were charged in 129 cases, for an average of 1.37 defendants per case; and in Fiscal Year 2005, 350 defendants were charged in 169 cases, for an average of 2.07 defendants per case.

Continued success in this area will take a sustained commitment. To that end, the Department of Justice issued guidance to all United States Attorneys encouraging them to prosecute more nationwide and international criminal organizations that commit intellectual property crimes.

Criminal Enforcement Recommendation #8

Enhance Training Programs for Prosecutors and Law Enforcement Agents

Recommendation: The Department of Justice should enhance programs to train prosecutors and law enforcement agents investigating intellectual property offenses.

STATUS: IMPLEMENTED

Explanation: Law enforcement must be able to adapt its methods to the changing nature of intellectual property crime, and there must be a sufficient number of trained prosecutors to respond to this growing threat. Counterfeiters and copyright infringers rapidly adapt to new security measures, swiftly modify communication techniques and distribution channels in response to enforcement actions, and constantly create novel methods to advance their criminal activities.

In the past year, the Department of Justice has enhanced its programs to train prosecutors and law enforcement agents investigating intellectual property offenses. For example, in January 2006, the Department of Justice conducted a five-day annual training conference for approximately 200 CHIP prosecutors in Albuquerque, New Mexico; a significant portion of that training conference was devoted to improving intellectual property prosecutions. Three months later, the Department of Justice conducted a three-day Intellectual Property Seminar for approximately 50 AUSAs and federal agents at the National Advocacy Center in Columbia, South Carolina. For the first time ever, a large portion of the course was devoted to hands-on network and technology training for online investigations.

Recognizing the importance of these training conferences and seminars, the Department of Justice has issued guidance to all United States Attorneys setting forth the training responsibilities of CHIP prosecutors and CHIP Units. The guidance stressed the responsibility of each United States Attorney and CHIP prosecutor to ensure that CHIP Coordinators maintain their expertise by attending conferences and seminars sponsored by the Department of Justice's Office of Legal Education, especially the annual CHIP conference and Intellectual Property Seminar. In addition, CHIP AUSAs were encouraged to conduct in-office legal training to keep other AUSAs apprised of critical search and seizure law applicable to obtaining electronic evidence and conducting electronic surveillance. Finally, CHIP prosecutors, especially those in CHIP Units, were directed to enhance regional training on intellectual property enforcement for federal and state agents, and to continue to conduct outreach to the high-tech industry and rights-holder sector to foster the sharing of information critical to effective prosecutions.

In June 2006, the Department of Justice also published a comprehensive resource manual on prosecuting intellectual property crimes. This nearly 400-page manual is an invaluable training resource for federal prosecutors and agents nationwide. It presents comprehensive descriptions and analysis on all the federal criminal intellectual property laws, including copyright, trademark, theft of trade secrets, and counterfeit labeling. It improves on earlier versions by adding broader and more in-depth coverage of all areas; fully identifying recent changes to the case law, statutes, and sentencing guidelines; and adding new chapters on the Digital Millennium Copyright Act, patent law, and victim issues.

The Department of Justice's training efforts have not been limited to the United States. Intellectual property theft and counterfeiting are global problems that require a strong and coordinated global enforcement response. Building relationships between American law enforcement and its counterparts overseas is essential to ensuring continued success in multi-national cases. Therefore, the Department of Justice has increased and improved its international training efforts as well. For example, in the last year alone,

Department of Justice prosecutors met with more than 2,000 prosecutors, investigators, judges, and intellectual property experts from 94 countries to provide training and technical assistance in intellectual property enforcement. These types of bilateral and multilateral outreach efforts help develop greater enforcement capacity in other countries, while also developing cooperative law enforcement contacts for better coordination on international protection of intellectual property rights.

Criminal Enforcement Recommendation #9

Prosecute Intellectual Property Offenses That Endanger the Public's Health or Safety

Recommendation: The Department of Justice should prosecute aggressively intellectual property offenses that endanger the public's health or safety.

STATUS: IMPLEMENTED AND ONGOING

Explanation: Intellectual property crime can pose a serious health and safety risk to the public, from faulty electrical cords to fake medicines and pesticides that can harm unsuspecting consumers. Although the Department of Justice has long prioritized the prosecution of intellectual property cases that place the public at risk, this prioritization had not previously been formally emphasized at the highest levels of the Department of Justice. Accordingly, the Department of Justice has issued guidance to all United States Attorneys emphasizing the importance of aggressively prosecuting intellectual property offenses that endanger the health and safety of the public.

The Department of Justice has also continued to work with federal, State, and local agencies that encounter these products at the Nation's borders and in the marketplace, and it has continued to prosecute those who endanger the public through intellectual property offenses. For example, in January 2005, a 58-year-old California man was convicted of conspiracy to import into the United States at least 50,000 counterfeit Viagra tablets manufactured in China, and conspiracy to manufacture another 700,000 tablets of counterfeit Viagra. The counterfeit Viagra was valued at over $5.6 million.

In August 2005, 11 individuals and three businesses were indicted in Missouri for participating in a $42 million conspiracy to sell counterfeit, illegally imported, and misbranded cholesterol medication (Lipitor) and other drugs and for participating in a conspiracy to sell stolen drugs.

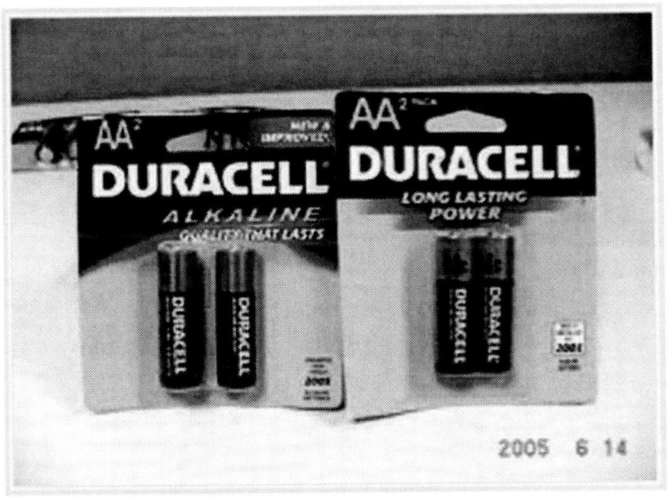

Counterfeit (left) and genuine batteries (right) discovered by United States Customs and Border Protection inspectors in Los Angeles, California. Photo by Dept. of Homeland Security, Immigration and Customs Enforcement.

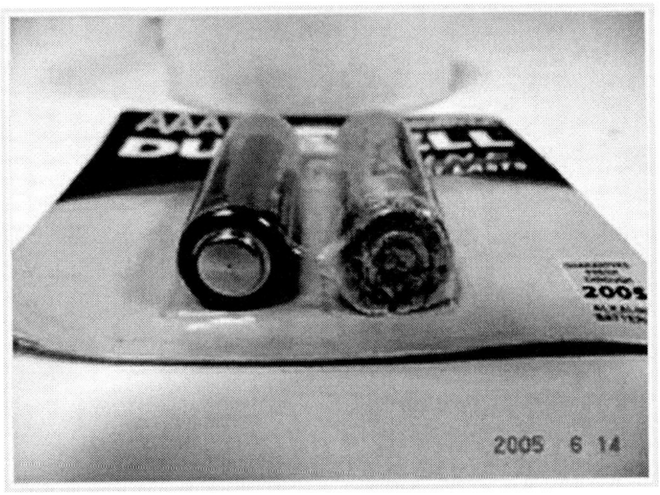

Corroded counterfeit batteries seized in Los Angeles, California by Special Agents of the United States Immigration and Customs Enforcement agency in June 2005. Photo by Dept. of Homeland Security, Immigration and Customs Enforcement.

In September 2005, as part of an ICE investigation known as Operation Ocean Crossing, a Washington man was indicted on charges of importing and distributing counterfeit pharmaceuticals from China. These charges arose from information provided by the ICE liaison in Beijing, China, regarding the online Internet site "*bestonlineviagra.com.*" The defendant owned and operated the Internet site in order to distribute bulk quantities of counterfeit Viagra and Cialis manufactured in China. In conjunction with the investigation of the defendant in the United States, agents assisted officials from the Ministry of Public Security and Public Security Bureau in China in determining the source of the counterfeit pharmaceutical drugs. The joint investigation resulted in Chinese authorities' arresting 11 individuals in China for manufacturing and distributing counterfeit Viagra, Cialis, and Lipitor. In February 2006, the defendant pleaded guilty in Houston to trafficking in counterfeit pharmaceuticals in violation of federal drug laws.

On May 25, 2006, the Department of Justice obtained a jury verdict against a licensed Texas pharmacist on charges of conspiring to import counterfeit drugs from China bearing the trademarks Viagra and Cialis, without authorization of the manufacturers and owners of those marks, Pfizer and Eli Lilly, and thereafter distributing the fake drugs to the public; trafficking in counterfeit goods; and misbranding and mislabeling drugs in violation of federal drug laws.

Criminal Enforcement Recommendation #10

Emphasize Charging Of Intellectual Property Offenses

Recommendation: The Department of Justice should emphasize the importance of charging intellectual property offenses in every type of investigation where such charges are applicable, including organized crime, fraud, and international smuggling.

STATUS: IMPLEMENTED AND ONGOING

Explanation: Many crimes involve intellectual property offenses. When the focus of the investigation centers on another serious offense, however, the intellectual property offenses are often not emphasized and sometimes not charged. For example, defendants who commit organized crime or fraud offenses that involve counterfeiting are usually charged with racketeering or fraud violations, sometimes without additional intellectual property charges. The Task Force recommended that the Department of Justice emphasize that intellectual property offenses should always be charged when appropriate, and that Department of Justice prosecutors should seek to convict defendants involved in intellectual property offenses regardless of whether the focus of the investigation is on another serious offense.

To implement this recommendation, the Department of Justice has issued guidance to all United States Attorneys that, among other things, emphasizes the importance of using the intellectual property statutes "to combat the burgeoning trade in counterfeit and infringing goods and digital property." The guidance directs that, whenever possible, United States Attorneys should charge and convict offenders of readily provable violations of the following core intellectual property statutes: criminal copyright infringement, 18 U.S.C. § 2319; trademark (counterfeit product) offenses, 18 U.S.C. § 2320; circumvention of copyright control systems in violation of the Digital Millennium Copyright Act, 17 U.S.C. §§ 1201-04; satellite signal piracy, 47 U.S.C. §§ 553, 605; economic espionage and theft of trade secrets, 18 U.S.C. §§ 1831-32; counterfeit labeling, 18 U.S.C. § 2318; live music infringement, 18 U.S.C. § 2319A; unauthorized recording of motion pictures, 18 U.S.C. § 2319B; and counterfeit drug offenses in violation of the Food, Drug and Cosmetic Act, 21 U.S.C. § 33 1(i).

Criminal Enforcement Recommendation #11

Enhance Victim Education Programs and Increase Cooperation

Recommendation: The Department of Justice should enhance its program of educating and encouraging victims of intellectual property offenses and industry representatives to cooperate in criminal investigations. Recommended enhancements include:

(1) Encouraging victims to report intellectual property crime to law enforcement agencies;
(2) Distributing the new "Department of Justicc Guide to Reporting Intellectual Property Crime" to victims and industry representatives regarding federal intellectual property offenses; and

(3) Hosting a conference with victims and industry representatives to educate participants on how they can assist in law enforcement investigations.

STATUS: IMPLEMENTED

Explanation: Combating intellectual property crime often requires cooperation among law enforcement, prosecutors, and victims of intellectual property theft. Information-sharing and prompt reporting by victims can be essential to the success of an investigation or prosecution; victims are often in the best position to detect immediately when their intellectual property has been stolen. Accordingly, in the past 18 months, the Department of Justice has taken a number of measures to encourage victim reporting and enhance cooperation.

First, the Department of Justice has been proactive in its outreach to industry and victims to encourage reporting of intellectual property crime. The Department of Justice has sought opportunities to partner with other federal agencies to educate and inform rights holders. For example, the Department of Justice participated in a series of six conferences organized by the USPTO on intellectual property basics for small- and medium-size businesses, entrepreneurs, and independent inventors. These two-day "Conference[s] on Intellectual Property in the Global Marketplace" were held in Austin, Texas; Miami, Florida; Phoenix, Arizona; San Diego, California; Salt Lake City, Utah; and Columbus, Ohio. They were designed to assist small business owners in learning about their rights and the new realities of intellectual property counterfeiting and piracy in the global marketplace. At each of these national conferences, local CHIP prosecutors gave presentations on federal criminal intellectual property enforcement, criminal statutes, case development, and cooperation with victims. Copies of the "Department of Justice Guide to Reporting Intellectual Property Crime" were distributed to small business owners and industry representatives in attendance.

Second, the Department of Justice was also proactive in organizing two of its own victim education conferences, each entitled "Counterfeit Goods: The Danger, The Crimes, The Victims." These one- day conferences in Los Angeles and New York City brought together private investigators from the manufacturing industry, company representatives, federal and State prosecutors, and federal, State, and local agents. Topics included how criminal cases are investigated and the types of evidence most useful to those investigations. A particular focus of the conferences was educating industry representatives and their investigators on the laws, regulations, Department of Justice directives, and rules of professional conduct that are implicated when victim companies offer assistance or seek to donate resources in connection with federal investigations.

Criminal Enforcement Recommendation #12

Issue Internal Guidance to Federal Prosecutors Regarding How Victims Can Assist Prosecutors in Intellectual Property Cases

Recommendation: The Department of Justice should issue internal guidance to federal prosecutors regarding how victims can assist prosecutors in intellectual property cases.

STATUS: IMPLEMENTED

Explanation: Prosecutions of intellectual property crime often depend on cooperation between victims and law enforcement. Without information from victims, prosecutors cannot enforce the intellectual property laws as effectively. Many industry groups and victims of intellectual property theft are eager to assist law enforcement in finding intellectual property offenders and bringing them to justice. Certain types of assistance, however, such as the donation of funds, property, or services by outside sources, can raise legal and ethical issues. In order to maintain the Department of Justice's independence and integrity, federal rules and regulations place limitations on the types of assistance victims and outside sources can provide to law enforcement authorities.

Additionally, the Department of Justice's newly published 400-page resource manual on "Prosecuting Intellectual Property Crimes" contains an in-depth section on offers of assistance from victims and related parties in intellectual property investigations and prosecutions. The manual advises Department of Justice prosecutors on applicable laws and regulations relating to the acceptance of gifts; the distinction between "gifts" and "assistance"; professional responsibility issues; and case-related concerns.

State and Federal intellectual property prosecutors at Victims' Conference in New York City on April 27, 2006. From the left: Asst. D.A. Gregory Pavlides (Queens D.A.'s Office); Asst. U.S. Attorney Jed Davis (Eastern Dist. of New York); Vice Chairman, Intellectual Property Task Force Arif Alikhan (U.S. Dept. of Justice); Asst. U.S. Attorney Joseph DeMarco (Southern Dist. of New York); Asst. D.A. Jeff Levinson (Manhattan D.A.'s Office); Asst. D.A. Richard Baker (Bronx D.A.'s Office); Asst. D.A. Tiana Walton (Manhattan D.A.'s Office); and Trial Attorney Matthew Bassiur (U.S. Dept. of Justice). Photo by Susan Butler.

B. International Cooperation Recommendations

The Task Force continues to believe that international cooperation is critical to stemming the tide of global intellectual property crime. Foreign governments must themselves prosecute intellectual property criminals and assist the United States in gathering evidence and prosecuting those who violate American intellectual property laws. Accordingly, in 2004, the Task Force recommended that the Department of Justice adopt the following recommendations regarding international cooperation. The status of each recommendation is set forth below.

> *"[T]he protection of intellectual property is among the powers expressly delegated to Congress by Article I of the Constitution in 1789. Those benefits are undermined, however, when other nations permit, whether overtly or tacitly, infringement on intellectual property rights."*
>
> - Associate Attorney General, Robert D. McCallum, Jr., March 2, 2006

(1) Deploy federal prosecutors to Hong Kong and Budapest, Hungary, and designate them as "Intellectual Property Law Enforcement Coordinators" ("IPLECs") to coordinate intellectual property enforcement efforts in those regions;

STATUS: IMPLEMENTED AND ONGOING

(2) Recommend that the FBI co-locate Legal Attachés with intellectual property expertise to Hong Kong and Budapest, Hungary, to assist the newly assigned IPLECs in investigative efforts;

STATUS: IMPLEMENTED AND ONGOING

(3) Direct prosecutors and agents to increase the use of alternative channels of communication, such as "law enforcement-to-law enforcement" contacts, to collect information and evidence quickly in foreign investigations;

STATUS: IMPLEMENTED AND ONGOING

(4) Enhance its intellectual property training programs for foreign prosecutors and law enforcement investigators in coordination with the Department of State;

STATUS: IMPLEMENTED

(5) Prioritize treaty negotiations for legal assistance agreements with foreign governments where intellectual property enforcement is a significant problem;

STATUS: IMPLEMENTED AND ONGOING

(6) Ensure that intellectual property crimes are included in all extradition treaties and prioritize negotiations with foreign countries according to intellectual property enforcement concerns; and

STATUS: IMPLEMENTED AND ONGOING

(7) Emphasize intellectual property enforcement issues during discussions with foreign governments.

STATUS: IMPLEMENTED AND ONGOING

Additional information regarding each of the recommendations and its status is set forth below.

International Cooperation Recommendation #1

Deploy Intellectual Property Law Enforcement Coordinators to Asia and Eastern Europe

Recommendation: The Department of Justice should deploy federal prosecutors to the United States consulate in Hong Kong and embassy in Budapest, Hungary, and designate them "Intellectual Property Law Enforcement Coordinators" ("IPLECs") to coordinate intellectual property enforcement efforts in those regions.

STATUS: IMPLEMENTED AND ONGOING

Explanation: The 2004 Report correctly forecast the expanding challenge of combating intellectual property crimes throughout the world and recommended that the Department of Justice deploy Intellectual Property Law Enforcement Coordinators (or "IPLECs") in Asia (Hong Kong) and Eastern Europe (Budapest, Hungary). In January 2006, a new Department of Justice attaché was assigned to the United States Embassy in Bangkok, Thailand. The Department of Justice used this existing resource to designate an IPLEC for the region. The attaché is an experienced intellectual property prosecutor who formerly led the CHIP Unit in Northern California. Since being designated the IPLEC for Asia, he has been successful in advancing the Department of Justice's regional intellectual property goals.

Since January 2006, the IPLEC has participated in intellectual property rights enforcement seminars and meetings in China, Hong Kong, Cambodia, Thailand, Taiwan, the Philippines, Indonesia, and Malaysia, and has additional visits planned to Korea, Japan, and Singapore. These meetings, whose participants have included foreign judges, prosecutors, investigators and other intellectual property officials, have allowed the Department of Justice to establish valuable contacts with regional counterparts and gather information about the unique intellectual property rights enforcement challenges confronting individual Asian countries. In presentations at these meetings, the IPLEC has highlighted the Department of Justice's successes in combating intellectual property crime, the benefits of specialized intellectual property prosecutorial and investigative units (*e.g.,* CHIP units and CCIPS), and the importance of international cooperation and coordinated, cross-border prosecutions. In the near future, the IPLEC will play an important role in programs to increase criminal enforcement of intellectual property laws in both China and India, two countries with enormous capacity to produce counterfeit and pirated goods and a history of damaging United States rights-holders by manufacturing infringing goods.

The IPLEC is also developing an Intellectual Property-Prosecution and Investigation Network ("IP- PIN") comprised of key intellectual property prosecutors and investigators from countries in the region. Intellectual property officials from several countries have already committed to participate in the network, which will better enable the sharing of information and strategies, help identify regional training opportunities, and facilitate coordinated prosecutions. The Department of Justice plans to host an IP-PIN conference within the next six to nine months to strengthen these important law enforcement relationships.

Recognizing that effective prosecution of intellectual property crime depends heavily on cooperation between victims and law enforcement authorities, the IPLEC has regularly met with regional industry representatives with extensive experience in intellectual property rights enforcement in Asia, including representatives from the Motion Picture Association and the Business Software Alliance, as well as pharmaceutical and other "hard good" industries. The IPLEC has also improved regional awareness of the Department of Justice's efforts to combat intellectual property crime by addressing the American Chamber of Commerce in Asian countries and by collaborating closely with representatives from the Departments of Commerce and State to promote interagency cooperation and better achieve the goals of the Bush Administration's STOP Initiative.

The Department of Justice has also secured agreement in principle from the Bureau for International Narcotics and Law Enforcement Affairs at the Department of State (subject to Congressional approval and approval of a budget and work plan) to provide start-up costs to support a full-time IPLEC for Eastern Europe for one year. The Department of Justice will begin interviewing experienced intellectual property prosecutors for the new IPLEC position in the next month. The Department of Justice will be responsible for the Eastern European IPLEC position after Fiscal Year 2007. The Department of Justice will work with the Department of State to identify an appropriate location for the IPLEC in the region.

International Cooperation Recommendation #2

Deploy FBI Legal Attachés To Assist IPLEC Investigative Efforts

Recommendation: The FBI should co-locate Legal Attachés with intellectual property expertise to Hong Kong and Budapest, Hungary, to assist the newly assigned IPLECs in investigative efforts.

STATUS: IMPLEMENTED AND ONGOING

Explanation: The Department of Justice has designated its legal attaché in Bangkok, Thailand, as the IPLEC to oversee the entire Asian region. Similarly, the FBI has a Legal Attaché and an Assistant Legal Attaché posted in Bangkok and attachés in Eastern Europe. Although these agents are assigned to investigate all FBI matters, they are available to assist the IPLEC in any intellectual property matters. The FBI also has personnel assigned in Beijing and Hong Kong, China; Kuala Lumpur, Malaysia; Manila, Philippines; Seoul, South Korea; Singapore; and Tokyo, Japan. In addition, the FBI has personnel assigned throughout Eastern Europe including in Bulgaria, Latvia, Romania and Russia. If additional resources are necessary for intellectual property investigations in these areas, FBI Headquarters is dedicated to providing agent support through temporary assignments as needed.

International Cooperation Recommendation #3

Increase the Use of Informal Contacts to Gather Evidence from Foreign Countries

Recommendation: Direct prosecutors and agents to increase the use of alternative channels of communication, such as "law enforcement-to-law enforcement" contacts, to collect information and evidence quickly in foreign investigations.

STATUS: IMPLEMENTED AND ONGOING

Explanation: As noted in the 2004 Report, international cooperation in the area of intellectual property crime often requires immediate action or the evidence may be lost. The Department of Justice continues to increase its network of worldwide contact points to allow for quick and direct communication in fast-moving investigations. Where appropriate, the Department of Justice encourages using informal channels of communication, outside formal Mutual Legal Assistance Treaties, to obtain information from overseas. One example of the Department of Justice's progress in this area is the increased emphasis on a "24/7 network" for immediate international assistance in computer crime cases. Each of the 43 countries that participates in this international network has designated a point of contact who can be reached in an urgent case at any hour. This 24/7 network is especially useful to preserve information and evidence stored on a computer in a foreign country that may disappear without quick action by foreign authorities. Building upon the success of the 24/7 network for the investigation of computer-based crimes, the Department of Justice is developing and updating an international directory of law enforcement officials with the authority to criminally enforce intellectual property laws.

The Department of Justice has also issued guidance to all United States Attorneys' Offices encouraging use of all available tools and informal federal law enforcement channels–including federal investigative agencies' foreign legal attachés stationed in-country–to establish communication and cooperation with our foreign counterparts.

International Cooperation Recommendation #4:

Increase International Law Enforcement Training on Intellectual Property

Recommendation: Enhance its intellectual property training programs for foreign prosecutors and law enforcement investigators in coordination with the Department of State.

STATUS: IMPLEMENTED AND ONGOING

Explanation: The Department of Justice has taken an active role in providing training and expertise to develop effective criminal intellectual property enforcement regimes around the world. With funds provided by the State Department's International Narcotics and Law Enforcement Bureau for intellectual property training, the Department of Justice has organized and participated in more than 20 international programs in fiscal years 2005 and 2006. Programs have included: the development of manuals for prosecutors and investigators in intellectual property cases (in Panama and Paraguay); programs designed to increase cooperation between law enforcement agencies (in Mexico and Brazil); and regional programs addressing specific problems, such as the production and distribution of counterfeit optical media (Hong Kong). In the last year, Department of Justice prosecutors have met with more than 2,000 prosecutors, investigators, judges, and intellectual property experts from 94 countries to provide training and technical assistance in intellectual property enforcement. Department of Justice prosecutors also regularly support United States Embassy programs on intellectual property, typically working with Economic Bureau Officers or Department of Justice Resident Legal Advisors to provide in-country training on intellectual property enforcement. Through these types of bilateral and multilateral efforts, the Department of Justice seeks to develop greater enforcement capacity in these countries while also developing necessary law enforcement contacts to better coordinate international protection of intellectual property rights.

International Cooperation Recommendation #5

Prioritize Negotiations for Legal Assistance Treaties

Recommendation: The Department of Justice should prioritize treaty negotiations for legal assistance agreements with foreign governments where intellectual property enforcement is a significant problem.

STATUS: IMPLEMENTED AND ONGOING

Explanation: The Department of Justice is pleased to report progress in the area of treaty negotiations since the publication of the 2004 Report. Significantly, more than a dozen countries have ratified the Council of Europe

Convention on Cybercrime, with ratification pending in over two dozen other countries. This Convention is the first international treaty that specifically addresses the subject of computer crime. Among its provisions is a requirement that countries criminalize intellectual property infringement. The Convention will strengthen intellectual property law enforcement by allowing the United States to better protect its intellectual property rights in an international environment. The United States Senate Committee on Foreign Relations has approved the Convention and ratification by the full Senate is pending. The Task Force continues to recommend that the full Senate ratify the Convention on Cybercrime as soon as possible.

The 2004 Report identified Asia as a region relevant to many United States intellectual property investigations. On April 7, 2006, the United States Senate gave its advice and consent to a new Mutual Legal Assistance Treaty with Japan. Negotiations with Japan on this treaty lasted over 10 years, ending in early 2003. The treaty was signed in August 2003. The Department of Justice is currently in treaty negotiations with other countries in Asia where intellectual property is a concern. In treaty negotiations, the Department of Justice deliberately raises intellectual property as an issue of significant importance.

In addition to treaties with Asian countries, extradition and mutual legal assistance agreements with the European Union that were signed in June 2003 are now closer to implementation. As anticipated, following signature of the agreements, technical negotiations took place between the United States and the European Union countries to conform the agreements to the terms of existing bilateral treaties and to address the situation in which there is no bilateral mutual legal assistance treaty in force. The United States-European Union agreements will enter into force when the bilateral instruments between the United States and all 25 European Union countries have been completed, signed, and approved by the United States Senate. The Department of Justice has executed these bilateral agreements to implement obligations of United States-European Union Mutual Legal Assistance and Extradition Agreements that ensure cooperation regarding intellectual property crimes with Austria, Belgium, Cyprus, the Czech Republic, Denmark, Estonia, Germany, Greece, Finland, France, Hungary, Ireland, Italy, Latvia, Lithuania, Luxembourg, Malta, the Netherlands, Portugal, Slovakia, Slovenia, Spain, Sweden, and the United Kingdom; and has completed negotiations with the remaining country of Poland. Like the treaty with Japan, these agreements with the European Union should improve cooperation in intellectual property and other criminal investigations.

"The list of countries cooperating in these efforts is long, but the Department is committed to building on these successes and achieving even greater global participation in the future. In the increasingly connected global economy, nothing short of a global effort will suffice."

- Attorney General Alberto R. Gonzales, November 10, 2005

International Cooperation Recommendation #6

Prioritize Negotiations and Include Intellectual Property Crimes in Extradition Treaties

Recommendation: The Department of Justice should ensure that intellectual property crimes are included in all extradition treaties and prioritize negotiations with countries according to intellectual property enforcement concerns.

STATUS: IMPLEMENTED AND ONGOING

Explanation: It is important to have effective international extradition treaties that include intellectual property offenses in order to promote global cooperative efforts. In treaty negotiations with countries where intellectual property crime is a concern, the Department of Justice specifically raises intellectual property rights to ensure that the treaty will cover this type of crime. Each year, the Department of Justice prioritizes treaty negotiations with countries according to law enforcement concerns, including intellectual property. As mentioned previously, the United States is progressing toward implementation of a new extradition agreement with the European Union and the Department of Justice continually seeks to enter into new treaties or update existing treaties with other countries. Accordingly, the Department of Justice has implemented this recommendation and continues to seek additional opportunities to engage foreign partners on intellectual property issues.

International Cooperation Recommendation #7

Emphasize Intellectual Property Enforcement During Discussions with Foreign Governments

Recommendation: The Department of Justice should emphasize intellectual property enforcement issues during discussions with foreign governments.

STATUS: IMPLEMENTED AND ONGOING

Explanation: The Department of Justice holds regular high-level meetings with foreign governments, both in Washington and abroad. In these meetings, Department of Justice officials discuss international cooperation in criminal matters, including intellectual property crime. For example, intellectual property law enforcement was a primary topic at the annual United States/China Joint Liaison Group on Law Enforcement ("JLG") meeting in June 2006 in Washington, D.C., and talks are continuing to establish an expert working group on intellectual property law enforcement within the JLG framework. Moreover, the Attorney General raised intellectual property issues directly with his Chinese counterparts during his trip to China in November 2005. He also discussed intellectual property with Germany's Minister of Justice, Brigitte Zypries, in Washington, D.C., in April 2006. Minister Zypries has taken an aggressive stance in Germany against the theft of intellectual property. In addition, the Attorney General has raised intellectual property law enforcement in high-level meetings with Pakistan, which has aggressively pursued the producers of pirated optical media, and Canada, which played a significant role combating online piracy in Operation Site Down.

The Department of Justice has also pursued many opportunities to address and emphasize the importance of intellectual property enforcement through the International Visitors program administered by the Department of Justice's Office of Overseas Prosecutorial Development, Assistance, and Training.

C. Civil Enforcement

The Department of Justice fights against the theft of intellectual property most visibly through its enforcement of the Nation's criminal laws. The successful defense of intellectual property rights, however, also requires vigorous enforcement by the owners of intellectual property through the civil justice system. In 2004, the Task Force made the following recommendation regarding the Department of Justice's efforts to protect intellectual property rights in the civil courts. Following are the recommendation and its status.

Civil Enforcement Recommendation

Support Civil Enforcement of Intellectual Property Laws by Owners of Intellectual Property Rights

Recommendation: The Department of Justice should assist private parties in enforcing civil laws that protect intellectual property owners against theft by supporting an effective statutory framework for such enforcement. When a court decision or lawsuit threatens the civil remedies available under federal law, the Department of Justice should defend in court all appropriate intellectual property protections and vigorously defend Congress's authority in protecting intellectual property rights.

STATUS: IMPLEMENTED AND ONGOING

Explanation: In October 2004, the Task Force recommended that the Department of Justice support civil enforcement of intellectual property laws by victims of intellectual property theft and defend in court all appropriate intellectual property protections.

Since the adoption of the recommendations by the Attorney General, the Department of Justice has filed numerous *amicus* briefs in matters in which the United States was not a party but desired to express its opinion in the Supreme Court and in appellate courts. In these ways the Department of Justice consistently supported the maintenance and implementation of robust intellectual property rights. The Department of Justice also intervened in appropriate cases to become a party to the litigation. These briefs and interventions promote legal precedents that enforce intellectual property rights fairly and consistently. By filing briefs in civil cases, the Department of Justice plays a vital role in promoting a legal environment that protects creativity and innovation.

Since October 2004, the Department of Justice has filed 13 *amicus* briefs in the Supreme Court in cases involving intellectual property rights, and more than a dozen *amicus* briefs and Statements of Interest (which are filed at the trial court and appellate court level) in such cases. These filings encompass all types of intellectual property, from pharmaceuticals to music and movies. In many of these cases, courts have adopted the arguments made by the Department of Justice and, consequently, expanded protections for owners of intellectual property rights. A description of some of these matters follows.

During an official visit to Beijing, China, Attorney General Alberto R. Gonzales meets with Chinese Communist Party Official, Luo Gan, on November 18, 2005, where he discusses the importance of intellectual property rights and enforcement. Photo by Carolyn Nelson.

A. Supreme Court Cases

- *Metro-Goldwyn-Mayer Studios Inc. v. Grokster,* 125 S. Ct. 2764 (2005):

In recent years, many individuals have used "file-sharing" software, such as "Grokster," to copy and distribute copyrighted music, movies, and software over the Internet without the authorization of the copyright owners. In this case, the Supreme Court addressed whether Grokster and other software providers could be held secondarily liable for copyright infringement.

The Department of Justice's *amicus* brief argued that the Court should examine Grokster's business plan and knowledge of likely infringement to determine whether Grokster could be liable for actively inducing users to infringe copyrights on its peer-to-peer network. The Department of Justice focused on evidence that Grokster intended to use the enticement of illegally copied music to generate advertising revenue.

The Supreme Court ultimately ruled against the software providers and adopted a liability standard that closely followed one of the standards proposed by the Department of Justice. This decision will help victims of intellectual property theft protect the value of their property from unauthorized online distribution by allowing lawsuits against those who may be secondarily liable for infringing the owner's rights.

- *eBay Inc. v. MercExchange,* LLC, 2006 WL 1310670 (May 15, 2006):

The *eBay* case was the subject of considerable press commentary about the role of intellectual property enforcement as it relates to innovation and, in particular, the standards that judges must use to grant a permanent injunction against a patent infringer.

On March 10, 2006, the Department of Justice filed an *amicus* brief regarding these standards. The Department of Justice argued in favor of a permanent injunction against the patent infringer and advocated a set of principles that should apply in such cases. On May 15, 2006, the Supreme Court issued a decision that adopted much of the Department of Justice's reasoning.

- *Illinois Tool Works, Inc. v. Independent Ink, Inc.,* 126 S. Ct. 1281 (2006):

The Nation's antitrust laws prohibit companies from using a monopoly in one market to establish a monopoly in another market, or in other words, from "tying" the sale of one product to the sale of another product. Oftentimes, a company will sue a patent holder under the antitrust laws and claim that the patent holder illegally "tied" the sale of another product to the patented product. As part of this claim, the company alleges that the patent's existence gives the patent holder an economic monopoly, or "market power," in a particular market.

In this case, the U.S. Court of Appeals for the Federal Circuit held that Supreme Court precedent established a rebuttable presumption that the defendant has such market power if the tying product is patented. The Supreme Court granted review, and the United States filed an *amicus* brief arguing both that controlling precedent did not mandate a presumption that patents confer market power and that such a presumption would conflict with the procompetitive policies of the antitrust laws. In a unanimous decision, the Supreme Court rejected the presumption and, as the United States had urged, vacated the Federal Circuit's judgment and remanded the case for further proceedings in the district court to determine, among other things, whether the defendant had market power.

- *McFarling v. Monsanto Co.*, 125 S. Ct. 2956 (2005):

In this case, a licensee had claimed that a patent owner committed patent misuse or related antitrust violations when it refused to permit the saving and replanting of second generation genetically-modified agricultural seeds. The Federal Circuit rejected the licensee's claim. On petition for certiorari before the U.S. Supreme Court, the United States, as amicus, stated that it is well-settled that "[a] patentee . . . does not engage in patent misuse when it merely invokes its core right to refuse to license its patented invention," and therefore, there was no need for the Supreme Court to review the Federal Circuit's decision. The Court agreed, denying the petition in June 2005.

- *Laboratory Corp. of America v. Metabolite Laboratories, Inc.*, No. 04-607:

The patent laws preclude patent protection for principles of nature, such as electricity and magnetism. Biotechnology inventions, however, often employ such discovered principles in methods of diagnosis.

In an *amicus* brief, the Department of Justice discussed the USPTO's recent guidelines regarding the circumstances in which the principles-of-nature doctrine will bar patent protection. The brief counseled the Court to exercise caution before broadly reviewing the principles-of-nature doctrine. As the brief argued, an overly broad application could jeopardize protection for a number of valuable patents on methods used to detect and treat various diseases. The brief also suggested a number of narrower rationales for resolving this particular case. A decision by the Supreme Court is expected in June 2006.

- *MedImmune, Inc. v. Genentech, Inc.*, No. 05-608:

The Declaratory Judgment Act generally permits parties having concrete disputes to obtain a judicial determination of their rights without having to run the risks that might flow from breaching a contract or infringing a patent.

However, the Federal Circuit has required a party to face a reasonable apprehension of an infringement suit in order to challenge a patent through a declaratory judgment action. The court has further held that a licensee who pays royalties under protest cannot file a declaratory judgment action because it lacks an apprehension that it will be sued. In an *amicus* brief, the Department of Justice has argued that the Federal Circuit's rule for patent cases is at odds with the general principles underlying the Declaratory Judgment Act, and that it impairs competition by prohibiting the party that may have the most interest in challenging a patent (a licensee) from bringing an action to have the patent declared invalid unless the licensee also breaches the license and incurs substantial risks. We expect that this case will be heard in the fall of 2006.

- *KSR International Co. v. Teleflex, Inc.,* No. 04-1350:

In this case, the Supreme Court has been asked to reverse a decision of the United States Court of Appeals for the Federal Circuit ("Federal Circuit") on the meaning of Section 103(a) of the patent laws and the use of prior art. That section prohibits patentability of an invention "if the differences between the subject matter sought to be patented and the prior art [*i.e.*, the preexisting state of knowledge in the relevant field] are such that the subject matter as a whole would have been obvious at the time the invention was made to a person having ordinary skill in the art to which said subject matter pertains." Prior art includes knowledge available to those skilled in the art through prior publications, patents, and products that have been sold or publicly used more than one year before the filing of a patent application. The Federal Circuit reversed a summary judgment that an adjustable automobile pedal patent was invalid because, in its view, the district court had not pointed to a specific suggestion in the prior art to combine features of two prior art devices. The petitioner contends that the suggestion test adds an element not contained in the statutory test for obviousness and is inconsistent with prior Supreme Court precedent. The Supreme Court has asked the Department of Justice for its views regarding the case.

- *Apotex Inc. v. Pfizer, Inc.,* No. 05-1006:

This case involves the circumstances in which companies that seek to market generic equivalents of patented brand-name drugs will be permitted to challenge the patents on the brand-name drug. In this case, the Court of

Appeals held that a prospective generic drug manufacturer could not sue a patent holder to obtain a judicial ruling that its generic drug would not infringe the patent, because there was no risk that the patent holder would sue for infringement in the near future. Petitioner contends that it should be permitted to obtain judicial confirmation that its generic drug would not infringe the patents in order to facilitate government approval. The Supreme Court has asked the Department of Justice for its views regarding this complex case.

- *Empresa Cubana del Tabaco d/b/a Cubatabaco v. Culbro Corp.*, 399 F.3d 462 (2d Cir. 2005):

In trademark law, the "famous marks doctrine" permits a foreign trademark owner to establish certain rights if the trademark has achieved a certain level of consumer recognition from sales in other countries. In this case, the court considered whether the Cuban embargo prevented a Cuban company from acquiring the rights to the COHIBA trademark by operation of the famous marks doctrine.

In an *amicus* brief, the Department of Justice argued that the embargo prevented the Cuban company from acquiring the mark, but did not prevent it from cancelling the United States mark that was previously awarded to another entity in the United States but was cancelled based on the Cuban entity's use of the mark abroad. A federal court of appeals agreed with the Department of Justice's analysis under the embargo, but disagreed that the Cuban entity could obtain a cancellation of the mark. The Supreme Court invited the Department of Justice to file a brief expressing the views of the United States, which was filed on May 19, 2006.

B. Lower Court Cases

- *DMCA subpoena litigation:*

Unfortunately, some Internet users illegally distribute copyrighted material over the Internet. The Digital Millennium Copyright Act ("DMCA") authorizes copyright owners to subpoena Internet Service Providers ("IS Ps") to learn the identity of the ISPs' subscribers. In several lawsuits, however, ISPs have argued that the DMCA does not apply to them if they merely serve as "conduits" to transmit infringing material, such as copyrighted music, and that if the DMCA does apply to them, it violates the Constitution.

In a number of cases, the Department of Justice intervened to defend copyright owners' use of civil subpoenas. The Department of Justice argued that the DMCA was constitutional and that it applied to ISPs who act as conduits. To date, courts generally have found that the DMCA does not reach conduit ISPs. Nevertheless, the Department of Justice continues to support the federal government's authority to enable private companies to combat copyright infringement by participating in appeals in these matters and intervening in lower court cases.

- *KISS Catalog v. Passport Int'l Productions, Inc.,* No. 03-CV-08514 (C.D. Cal. Dec. 21, 2005):

In this case, the rock band KISS sued a company for distributing an unauthorized recording of a 1976 concert. The Department of Justice intervened in the lawsuit and argued that an anti-bootlegging statute barred the company's unauthorized distribution. In its brief, the Department of Justice argued that the anti-bootlegging statute was valid because it fell outside the domain of the Copyright Clause's time limits on copyright protection, which apply to "writings" of an author. The court agreed with the Department of Justice's position, and held that the anti-bootlegging statute addresses live performances and unauthorized recordings rather than the "writings" of an author and serves to complement, rather than violate, the Copyright Clause. The court's decision expands the scope of intellectual property protection.

- *Aharonian v. Gonzales,* No. 04-5090 (District Court), No. 06-15361 (on appeal in the Ninth Circuit Court of Appeals):

The plaintiff, a computer programmer, sued the Department of Justice to block the enforcement of copyright laws against persons who copy computer source code. The plaintiff argues that the copyright laws are unconstitutionally vague as applied to source code. The plaintiff also argues that patent law, rather than copyright law, is the sole source of protection for intellectual property in computer programs. The Department of Justice is defending the suit on the ground that copyright laws clearly apply to computer programs and are not unconstitutionally vague. The district court ruled in the Department's favor, and the Department is now defending the district court's decision on appeal.

- *Elektra Entertainment Group, Inc. v. Barker,* No. 05-CV-7340 (S.D.N.Y.):

In this case, a peer-to-peer system user allegedly posted copies of recorded songs online and, thus, transferred those copies when they were downloaded by other system users. The defendant argued that electronically transferring a copy of a song was not the same thing as "distributing" the song within the meaning of the relevant statute. On April 21, 2006, the Department of Justice filed a Statement of Interest arguing that when a peer-to-peer system user electronically transfers a copy of a copyrighted file without authorization, that user infringes the copyright owner's distribution right. The Department of Justice's position, which comports with a number of court decisions, serves as a basis for many of the Department of Justice's criminal copyright infringement prosecutions. A decision is pending on the defendant's motion to dismiss.

- *Fonovisa, Inc. v. Alvarez,* No. 06-CV-01 1 (N.D. Tex.):

This case, like *Elektra Entertainment*, also involved a claim of peer-to-peer transfer of copyrighted works in which the defendant raised the same argument that an electronic transfer of a song did not constitute an infringing "distribution." On May 16, 2006, the Department of Justice filed a Statement of Interest advancing the same arguments as it did in the *Elektra Entertainment* case.

D. Antitrust Recommendations

The Antitrust Division's mission is to enforce federal antitrust laws. However, intellectual property plays an increasingly important role in the Antitrust Division's merger and civil non-merger investigations, and the Department of Justice bears in mind that the antitrust and intellectual property laws share the common purpose of promoting innovation and enhancing consumer welfare. The Department of Justice recognizes that enforcing antitrust laws in a way that condemns beneficial uses of intellectual property rights could undermine pro-competitive incentives.

Given the importance of the antitrust enforcement to the protection of intellectual property rights, Task Force made the following recommendations listed below. The status of each recommendation is also indicated below.

(1) Support the rights of intellectual property owners to decide independently whether to license their technology to others.

STATUS: IMPLEMENTED AND ONGOING

(2) Encourage trade associations and other business organizations seeking to establish industry standards for the prevention of intellectual property theft to use the Department of Justice's business review procedure for guidance regarding antitrust enforcement concerns.

STATUS: IMPLEMENTED AND ONGOING

(3) Continue to promote international cooperation and principled agreement between nations on the proper application of antitrust laws to intellectual property rights.

STATUS: IMPLEMENTED AND ONGOING

Detailed background information and an explanation of the status of each recommendation is set forth below.

Antitrust Recommendation #1

Support the rights of intellectual property owners to determine independently whether to license their technology.

Recommendation: The Department of Justice should support the rights of intellectual property owners to decide independently whether to license their technology to others.

STATUS: IMPLEMENTED AND ONGOING

Explanation: As its primary implementation of this recommendation, the Department of Justice ensures that its own antitrust enforcement efforts do not impair the important right of intellectual property owners to decide whether to license that property. In addition, the Department of Justice advocates frequently, before both domestic and international audiences, that this policy should exist throughout the world. The Department of Justice's Assistant Attorney General for Antitrust delivered a keynote address at the European Union Competition Workshop in June 2005 in which he stressed the importance of licensing freedom, tracing the development of this principle through United States Supreme Court precedent and comparing it to developing doctrines of law in the European Union. In addition, the Department of Justice has argued to uphold this principle in *amicus* briefs in several civil cases, as explained previously in this Progress Report.

Given the many Supreme Court cases indicating that the right to exclude is a fundamental right embodied in the grant of a patent, the Department of Justice has concluded that the right of intellectual property owners to unilaterally, unconditionally refuse to license a valid patent is clear. The Department of Justice will continue to focus on international advocacy, particularly in foreign jurisdictions that adopt a contrary view, for its future implementation of this recommendation.

Antitrust Recommendation #2

Encourage the use of the Justice Department's business review procedure.

Recommendation: The Department of Justice should encourage trade associations and other business organizations seeking to establish industry standards for the prevention of intellectual property theft to use the Justice Department's business review procedure for guidance regarding antitrust enforcement concerns.

STATUS: IMPLEMENTED AND ONGOING

Explanation: The Department of Justice promotes the use of its business review procedure through individual contact with interested parties and through various outreach efforts, including Internet resources. The Department of Justice maintains an Internet site that explains the business review procedure in detail (www.usdoj.gov/atr/public/busreview/procedure.htm) and provides searchable copies of business review letters issued since 1992. In addition, since the issuance of the 2004 Report, Department of Justice representatives, including the Assistant Attorney General for Antitrust, have encouraged industry to use the business review process through more than a dozen speeches and presentations that discuss the Task Force's recommendations.

Several intellectual property owners, both individually and as members of trade associations or other organizations, have begun preliminary discussions with the Department of Justice about the antitrust implications of their planned efforts to protect intellectual property rights, and may submit business review requests in the future. The Department of Justice treats pending business reviews as ongoing investigations and therefore does not recount the specifics of such requests to the public.

Antitrust Recommendation #3

Promote international cooperation on the application of antitrust laws to intellectual property rights.

Recommendation: The Department of Justice should continue to promote international cooperation and principled agreement between nations on the proper application of antitrust laws to intellectual property rights.

STATUS: IMPLEMENTED AND ONGOING

Explanation: The Department of Justice promotes sound intellectual property and competition policy through a variety of efforts under the coordination of its Antitrust Division's Foreign Commerce Section, assisted by the National Criminal Enforcement, Appellate, and Legal Policy Sections of the Antitrust Division and other Department of Justice components as appropriate. These efforts fall within several categories, including:

Intellectual Property Working Groups. Since the issuance of the 2004 Report, the Department of Justice has continued to engage in a number of intellectual property working groups, as well as more informal consultations, with the antitrust agencies of major United States trading partners. These agencies include the Japanese Fair Trade Commission, the Korean Fair Trade Commission, the Canadian Competition Bureau, and the Federal Competition Commission of Mexico. Throughout 2005 and 2006, the Department of Justice held meetings with representatives of the People's Republic of China, Chinese academics, and United States and Chinese business persons regarding China's efforts to enact its first general antitrust statute. In those meetings and in subsequent discussions, the Department of Justice has recommended that China's new law reflect the importance of ensuring that intellectual property rights are respected in order to foster the investment in innovation necessary for a competitive and dynamic market. The Department of Justice also meets on a frequent, informal basis with representatives of European nations and the European Union, including the Competition Directorate General of the European Commission, to discuss particular investigations and general principles involving competition law and intellectual property. In each of these efforts, the Department of Justice has worked jointly with the Bureau of Competition of the United States Federal Trade Commission.

Competition Advocacy through Multinational Organizations, Policy Forums, and Direct Training of Foreign Competition Agencies. The Department of Justice incorporates the promotion of sound intellectual property principles into its participation in numerous international conferences devoted to competition policy and economic growth. The Department of Justice helped found the International Competition Network ("ICN") in 2001 to promote effects-based competition laws worldwide and the principled convergence of antitrust analysis. The Department of Justice emphasized the protection of intellectual property rights at the June 2005 and May 2006 meetings of the ICN. The Department of Justice chairs the Working Party on Competition and Enforcement of the Competition Committee of the Organization for Economic Cooperation and Development and has advocated sound intellectual property policy in that forum throughout various meetings in 2005 and 2006. The Department of Justice regularly promotes the view that intellectual property and antitrust laws are complementary in speeches to public-private forums around the globe. In addition, it frequently provides guidance to foreign antitrust authorities seeking to create or revise their own intellectual property and antitrust enforcement policies and guidelines. Moreover, the Antitrust Division has had an active technical assistance program for many years through which it has advised governments in the process of adopting competition laws and new competition agencies on a wide range of antitrust issues, including the interplay between competition policy and intellectual property. In 2005-06, the recipients of such missions included Egypt, India, Russia, and several Latin American and Southeast Asian nations. Of particular interest, the current Assistant Attorney General for Antitrust visited authorities in China in June 2005, and the Antitrust Division's Deputy Assistant Attorney General for International Enforcement, Appellate, and Legal Policy visited China in May 2005 and March and May 2006. In many of these efforts, the Department of Justice coordinated its intellectual property policy and competition advocacy efforts with the Bureau of Competition of the United States Federal Trade Commission, and in some cases the Department of Justice also coordinated its efforts with the Competition Directorate General of the European Commission.

E. Prevention Recommendations

Education is a key tool in Department of Justice's mission to promote intellectual property protection. Protecting intellectual property is a collective effort of all citizens and therefore the public must be aware of their individual responsibilities. Therefore, the Department of Justice is constantly exploring opportunities to educate the public about intellectual property laws and the role that the Department of Justice plays in enforcement of those laws. In addition, the Department of Justice continues to form partnerships with victims of intellectual property theft in common educational initiatives. The Department of Justice has forged important, long-term partnerships with federal agencies, nonprofit educational institutions, and network television, with the goal of educating students and adults about the importance of protecting creativity through the development of educational programs and materials for classroom use. Accordingly, the recommendations set forth below were designed to increase the Department of Justice's effectiveness in preventing intellectual property crimes from occurring and raising public awareness. The status of each recommendation is set forth below.

(1) Develop a national education program to prevent intellectual property crime.

(A) Developing materials for student educational programs;

STATUS: IMPLEMENTED AND ONGOING

(B) Creating partnerships with non-profit educational organizations to promote public awareness regarding intellectual property crimes;

STATUS: IMPLEMENTED AND ONGOING

(C) Developing a video to teach students about the negative consequences of intellectual property theft; and

STATUS: IMPLEMENTED AND ONGOING

(2) Educate the public regarding the Department of Justice's policy on peer-to-peer networks.

STATUS: IMPLEMENTED

(3) Promote authorized use and awareness of the FBI's new anti-piracy seal and warning.

STATUS: IMPLEMENTED AND ONGOING

Prevention Recommendation #1

Develop a National Education Program to Prevent Intellectual Property Crime

Recommendation: The Department of Justice should develop a national program to educate students about the value of intellectual property and the consequences of committing intellectual property crimes by: (A) developing materials for student educational programs, (B) creating partnerships with non-profit educational organizations to promote public awareness regarding intellectual property crime, (C) developing a video to teach students about the negative consequences of intellectual property theft, and (D) encouraging federal prosecutors handling intellectual property crime cases throughout the nation to promote the Department of Justice's public awareness programs.

STATUS: IMPLEMENTED AND ONGOING

Explanation: The Department of Justice has developed strategic partnerships with non-profit educational organizations and other federal agencies to create and fund development of educational curricula, conduct educational events for students to learn interactively, and fund long-term teacher training programs.

National Educational Prevention Teacher Training Initiative

In a joint venture, the USPTO and the Department of Justice are funding a three-year, $300,000 annual program with three national nonprofit educational organizations: Street Law, i-Safe, and the Constitutional Rights Foundation. The program will focus on training teachers (who in turn will train other teachers) about intellectual property, the laws protecting it, and the responsibilities of citizens to respect it. The program will select major cities across the country to develop teacher-training seminars where teachers will be instructed about intellectual property by education experts, a network of local professional volunteer lawyers, federal investigators; federal prosecutors, and curriculum developers. Teachers will take their experience and knowledge back into the classroom and, with the curriculum developed by the nonprofit educational organization i-Safe, students will be taught about intellectual property and the importance of respecting it. The program also contemplates developing a website with free downloadable materials, games, and links to other Department of Justice intellectual property educational and outreach activities.

In October 2004, the Department of Justice formed an educational partnership with Street Law, i-Safe, and Court TV, with the goal of developing a national campaign aimed at educating students about intellectual property protection. One part of the national campaign involved creating a series of educational events entitled "Activate Your Mind: Protect Your Ideas" ("AYM"). The AYM campaign conducted a series of educational events throughout the country involving students, teachers, high-level government representatives, and victims of intellectual property theft. The AYM events were filmed by Court TV and broadcast on their educational series entitled "Choices and Consequences," which targets thousands of middle school and high school students across the country. The Court TV footage also served as material for an educational DVD to be used in conjunction with curriculum materials and public awareness events. The weeks leading up to the event cre-ated an opportunity for i-Safe and Street Law to introduce a curriculum to the participating students of the AYM events in an effort to educate and raise the student's level of awareness about intellectual property.

Activate Your Mind: Protect Your Ideas

Attorney General Alberto R. Gonzales participates in the second installment of Court TV's "Activate Your Mind: Protect Your Ideas" program on April 28, 2005 at UCLA with over 120 high school students to discuss movie and television piracy and the importance of protecting creativity. Photo courtesy of Court TV.

The first AYM event was held in October 2004 in Washington, D.C., at the Department of Justice and involved 100 area high school students. With a focus on music piracy, the event included presentations by songwriters, Department of Justice officials, victim representatives, a convicted intellectual property felon, on the impact of piracy.

On April 28, 2005, Attorney General Gonzales participated in the second installment of the AYM program at UCLA, with over 120 high school students, to discuss movie and television piracy and the importance of protecting creativity. The Attorney General led students in a question and answer session and students also heard from a convicted intellectual property offender, Assistant United States Attorneys, FBI agents, actors, stuntmen, and the President of the Motion Picture Association of America.

The third AYM event was held in March 2006 in San Jose and involved 100 middle school children. The Department of Justice partnered with the USPTO, Court TV, and Web Wise Kids (child internet safety experts), to discuss intellectual property. Focusing on software piracy, the educational partners used computer tools and programs to teach the students about intellectual property. The students then designed their own intellectual property software. An Assistant United States Attorney also educated the children about intellectual property laws. The students heard from, and interacted with, the Attorney General, the Director of the USPTO, and victim-industry representatives from the Electronic Software Alliance.

Attorney General Alberto R. Gonzales greets cheering students at the Windmill Springs Middle School on March 30, 2006 in San Jose, California where he participated in an educational event focused on intellectual property protection. Photo courtesy of Court TV.

Intellectual Property Forum

In October 2005, Attorney General Gonzales joined Commerce Secretary Carlos Gutierrez, Senator John Cornyn, and Congressman Lamar Smith at the University of Texas Law School in Austin, Texas, to discuss intellectual property with legal scholars and high-tech industry leaders. The panelists discussed the importance of the criminal and civil enforcement of intellectual property for future economic growth and innovation. This event was filmed by Court TV and incorporated into its educational programming that aired as part of its "Choices and Consequences" series. Copies of the program will be disseminated in conjunction with the Department of Justice's educational package for classrooms.

International Outreach

European countries have expressed interest in the efforts of the Department of Justice to prevent intellectual property theft through education. Department of Justice officials have traveled to various countries to participate in, and showcase, the strategies behind the efforts of the Department of Justice. Italy invited the Department of Justice and its educational partners to share, with high-level Italian officials, the Department of Justice's model of private sector and public cooperation in educational outreach. Similarly, French government officials invited the Department of Justice to share law enforcement strategies on educating the public about intellectual property theft and, as a result of the Attorney General's meeting with the Justice Minister of Germany, the Department is pursuing a partnership with German officials on intellectual property strategies for educational efforts.

Industry Outreach

In partnership with the United States Chamber of Commerce's Coalition Against Counterfeiting and Piracy ("CACP"), the Department of Justice has developed a working group of federal, State, and local prosecutors, investigators, and law enforcement officials to address the problems facing intellectual property enforcement and the importance of intellectual property victim-industry referrals. This working group participated in two conferences and invited intellectual property victim-industry members to attend. The purpose of the conferences was to explain the various aspects of intellectual property investigations for federal, state, and local enforcement and develop a better understanding among intellectual property victims of how to refer an intellectual property theft to law enforcement. The first conference was held in Los Angeles on March 7, 2006, and involved participants from the Los

Angeles Police Department, the Los Angeles Sheriff's Office, the Los Angeles District Attorney's Office, ICE, the FBI, and prosecutors from the United States Attorney's Office for the Central District of California.

The second conference was held in New York City in April 2006, and involved members from the New York Police Department's Trademark Infringement Group, the New York County District Attorney's office, the Bronx District Attorney's office, the Queens District Attorney's office, ICE, the FBI, United States Secret Service, and the United States Attorneys' Offices for the Eastern and Southern Districts of New York. The conference involved over 130 law enforcement and industry participants.

Prevention Recommendation #2

Educate the Public Regarding the Department of Justice's Policy on Peer-to-Peer Networks

Recommendation: The Department of Justice should educate the public regarding its policy prohibiting the use of peer-to-peer file-sharing networks on Justice Department computer systems.

U.S. government officials joined together to discuss the importance of intellectual property protection in the high-tech industry at the University of Texas Law School in Austin, Texas on October 31, 2005. Photographed from left to right are: Secretary Carlos Gutierrez, Department of Commerce, Attorney General Alberto R. Gonzales, U.S. Senator John Cornyn (R-Texas), and U.S. Rep. Lamar Smith (R-Texas). Photo courtesy of Court TV.

STATUS: IMPLEMENTED

Explanation: On September 17, 2004, the Department of Justice's Chief Information Officer issued a memorandum (contained in the Appendices of the 2004 Report) discussing the policy prohibiting the use of peer-to-peer software on its computer system. Since that time, the Department of Justice has distributed several thousand copies of the 2004 Report of the Department of Justice's Task Force on Intellectual Property to the public.

Prevention Recommendation #3

Promote Authorized Use and Awareness of the FBI's New Anti-Piracy Seal and Warning

Recommendation: The Department of Justice should promote authorized use and awareness of the FBI's new Anti-Piracy Seal to deter copyright infringement and trademark offenses.

STATUS: IMPLEMENTED AND ONGOING

Explanation: The Department of Justice has heavily promoted the use of the FBI's Anti-Piracy Seal to industry associations. Currently, the FBI has written agreements with the Motion Picture Association of America, the Recording Industry Association of America, the Software Information Industry Association, and the Entertainment Software Association, which use the Anti-Piracy Seal on copyrighted works to serve as a visible warning of the consequences of committing intellectual property crimes. The Department of Justice will continue to promote the use of the Anti-Piracy Seal with industry association representatives.

In: DOJ Progress Report on Intellectual Property ISBN: 978-1-60741-001-0
Editor: Todd B. Parker

Chapter 8

CONCLUSION

Department of Justice

The Department of Justice has implemented all of the recommendations contained in the 2004 Report. In addition, the Department of Justice has proposed and implemented additional recommendations to promote intellectual property rights. Notwithstanding these achievements, the Department of Justice will not cease its efforts. The Department of Justice will continue to increase its effectiveness in protecting the creativity and innovation that drives our Nation's economy. As indicated throughout this Progress Report, and in statements by the Attorney General, the theft of intellectual property is a threat to our national economic security. The Department of Justice will continue to wage an aggressive campaign to protect the Nation's intellectual resources.

In: DOJ Progress Report on Intellectual Property ISBN: 978-1-60741-001-0
Editor: Todd B. Parker

Chapter 9

Appendix A. Department of Justice Task Force on Intellectual Property: Summary of Recommendations

Department of Justice

A. Criminal Enforcement Recommendations

The Task Force has determined that protection of intellectual property is essential to maintain the nation's economic national security. Accordingly, the recommendations re-emphasize the Department of Justice's commitment to enforce aggressively the laws against the theft of copyrighted works, trademark counterfeiting, theft of trade secrets, and other intellectual property offenses. Accordingly, the recommendations set forth below are designed to strengthen the Department's commitment to protect intellectual property.

(1) The Department of Justice should create five additional CHIP Units in regions of the country where intellectual property producers significantly contribute to the national economy. These areas are the District of Columbia; Sacramento, California; Pittsburgh, Pennsylvania; Nashville, Tennessee; and Orlando, Florida;

(2) The Department of Justice should reinforce and expand existing CHIP Units located in key regions where intellectual property offenses have

increased, and where the CHIP Units have effectively developed programs to prosecute CHIP-related cases, coordinate law enforcement activity, and promote public awareness programs;

(3) The Department of Justice should designate CHIP Coordinators in every federal prosecutor's office and make the coordinators responsible for intellectual property enforcement in that region;

(4) The Department of Justice should examine the need to increase resources for the Computer Crime and Intellectual Property Section of the Criminal Division in Washington, D.C., to address additional intellectual property enforcement concerns;

(5) The Department of Justice should recommend that the FBI increase the number of Special Agents assigned to intellectual property investigations, as the Justice Department itself increases the number of prosecutors assigned to intellectual property enforcement;

(6) The Department of Justice should recommend that the FBI increase the number of personnel assigned to search for digital evidence in intellectual property cases;

(7) The Department of Justice should dismantle and prosecute more nationwide and international criminal organizations that commit intellectual property crimes;

(8) The Department of Justice should enhance programs to train prosecutors and law enforcement agents investigating intellectual property offenses;

(9) The Department of Justice should prosecute aggressively intellectual property offenses that endanger the public's health or safety;

(10) The Department of Justice should emphasize the importance of charging intellectual property offenses in every type of investigation where such charges are applicable, including organized crime, fraud, and illegal international smuggling;

(11) The Department of Justice should enhance its program of educating and encouraging victims of intellectual property offenses and industry representatives to cooperate in criminal investigations.

Recommended enhancements include:

(A) Encouraging victims to report intellectual property crime to law enforcement agencies;

(B) Distributing the new "Department of Justice Guide to Reporting Intellectual Property Crime" to victims and industry representatives regarding federal intellectual property offenses; and

(C) Hosting a conference with victims and industry representatives to educate participants on how they can assist in law enforcement investigations.

(12) The Department of Justice should issue internal guidance to federal prosecutors regarding how victims can assist prosecutors in intellectual property cases.

B. INTERNATIONAL COOPERATION RECOMMENDATIONS

International cooperation is a critical component in stemming the tide of global intellectual property theft. Intellectual property thieves in foreign countries must be subject to, and prosecuted by, foreign governments. In addition, foreign governments must assist the United States in its efforts to gather evidence and prosecute intellectual property criminals who violate the laws of the United States. Accordingly, the following recommendations are designed to increase cooperation with foreign countries regarding intellectual property enforcement:

(1) The Department of Justice should deploy federal prosecutors to the United States embassies in Hong Kong and Budapest, Hungary, and designate them as "Intellectual Property Law Enforcement Coordinators" ("IPLECs") to coordinate intellectual property enforcement efforts in those regions;

(2) The Department of Justice should recommend that the FBI co-locate Legal Attachés with intellectual property expertise to Hong Kong and Budapest, Hungary, to assist the newly assigned IPLECs in investigative efforts;

(3) Direct prosecutors and agents to increase the use of alternative channels of communication, such as "law enforcement-to-law enforcement" contacts, to collect information and evidence quickly in foreign investigations;

(4) The Department of Justice should enhance its intellectual property training programs for foreign prosecutors and law enforcement investigators in coordination with the Department of State;

(5) The Department of Justice should prioritize treaty negotiations for legal assistance agreements with foreign governments where intellectual property enforcement is a significant problem;

(6) The Department of Justice should ensure that intellectual property crimes are included in all extradition treaties and prioritize negotiations with foreign countries according to intellectual property enforcement concerns; and

(7) The Department of Justice should emphasize intellectual property enforcement issues during discussions with foreign governments.

C. Civil Enforcement Recommendation

The Department of Justice fights against the theft of intellectual property most visibly through its enforcement of the Nation's criminal laws. The successful defense of intellectual property rights, however, also requires vigorous enforcement by the owners of intellectual property through the civil justice system. In 2004, the Task Force made the following recommendation regarding the Department of Justice's efforts to protect intellectual property rights in the civil courts.

(1) The Department of Justice should assist private parties in enforcing civil laws that protect intellectual property owners against theft by supporting an effective statutory framework for such enforcement. When a court decision or lawsuit threatens the civil remedies available under federal law, the Justice Department should defend in court all appropriate intellectual property protections and vigorously defend Congress's authority in protecting intellectual property rights.

D. ANTITRUST RECOMMENDATIONS

The Department of Justice's Antitrust Division is responsible for promoting and protecting the competitive process and the American economy through enforcement of antitrust laws. These laws prohibit a variety of practices that restrain trade, such as price-fixing conspiracies, corporate mergers likely to reduce competition, and predatory acts designed to achieve or maintain monopoly power. When these practices involve intellectual property, they can raise complex questions about the proper application of antitrust to intellectual property rights. The Task Force Report recognizes that intellectual property rights can promote competition by creating incentives to innovate and commercialize new ideas that enhance consumer welfare and that enforcing the antitrust laws in a way that condemns the beneficial use of intellectual property rights could undermine the incentive to create and disseminate intellectual property. The following recommendations help ensure that the antitrust laws are appropriately applied to intellectual property in a way that does not chill the exercise of legitimate intellectual property rights:

(1) The Department of Justice should support the rights of intellectual property owners to decide independently whether to license their technology to others;

(2) The Department of Justice should encourage trade associations and other business organizations seeking to establish industry standards for the prevention of intellectual property theft, to use the Justice Department's business review procedure for guidance regarding antitrust enforcement concerns; and

(3) The Department of Justice should continue to promote international cooperation and principled agreement between nations on the proper application of antitrust laws to intellectual property rights.

E. Legislative Recommendations

The Task Force examined a number of pending bills in Congress and developed a set of general principles to guide pending and future legislation regarding the enforcement of intellectual property rights.

Principles for Pending Legislation

The circumvention of technological safeguards protecting copyrighted works should be subject to prosecution. The owners of intellectual property have the primary responsibility for protecting their creative works from unauthorized duplication. Technological safeguards such as digital rights management software and other forms of copy-protection provide means of doing so. Federal law should reinforce the use of these technological safeguards by preventing their deliberate and unauthorized circumvention.

The distribution of counterfeit products should be thwarted by seizing, when possible, the materials and equipment used in making them. The distribution of counterfeit products (both goods and creative works) represents not only a theft of intellectual property and a potential source of consumer fraud, but a significant threat to public health and safety. In order to prevent the distribution of counterfeit products, the government should take reasonable steps to prevent their production. When law enforcement officials find materials and equipment used to create counterfeit products, materials and equipment should be seized. Legal loopholes should not allow trafficking counterfeit labels because they have not yet attached to counterfeit goods.

The passive sharing of copyrighted works for unlawful duplication should be treated as the distribution of those works and should, where appropriate, be subject to prosecution. Distributing unauthorized copies of copyrighted works is a criminal violation if the total retail value of the original work, multiplied by the number of unauthorized copies, reaches a certain monetary threshold. Given the minimal cost of distributing copyrighted works over the Internet, making such files available for others to copy is equivalent to distributing them. The criminal copyright statute should therefore prohibit people from knowingly making available to the public a threshold number of infringing copies or exceeding a threshold value.

Copyright law should recognize the premium value of a copyrighted work before the work is released for sale to the general public. A copy of a copyrighted work is more valuable before it can be legitimately obtained by anyone else. In such situations, not only is this "prerelease" copy rarer, but it can also permit the holder to distribute copies as early as – or before – the copyrighted work's legitimate owner. As a result, although prerelease copies of a copyrighted work have no legitimate retail value, they can be the most valuable copies of all and their distribution can damage the rights holder. The copyright laws should reflect the premium value of pre-release copies, particularly at the stage of sentencing defendants for criminal violations.

The law should provide a remedy against those who intentionally induce infringement. Owners of intellectual property have the primary responsibility for protecting their intellectual property through civil enforcement actions if necessary. Computer networks that facilitate the unauthorized sharing and copying of copyrighted works by users are some of the most dangerous threats to copyright ownership today. A copyright owner should have some express remedy against such networks and other businesses, to the extent that they depend upon and intend for their customers to violate the owner's copyright.

Principles for Future Legislation

The law should prohibit not only the sale of counterfeit goods, but also the possession of counterfeit goods with the intent to sell them. Under current law, it is illegal to sell counterfeit goods (or to attempt to do so), but it is not illegal to possess even large quantities of counterfeit goods with the intention of selling them. As a result, someone who is caught with a warehouse full of counterfeit handbags may escape prosecution for trademark violations if there is no evidence that he has already sold or attempted to sell them. The Task Force recommended further consideration of a proposal to criminalize the possession of counterfeit goods with the intention of selling or otherwise trafficking in them.

The law should not distinguish between selling counterfeit goods for cash and giving them away with the general expectation of receiving any other type of benefit in the future. Under current trademark law, it is a criminal violation to sell or traffic in counterfeit goods. At least one court has held, however, that it is not illegal to give away such goods where there is no agreement to get something of value from the recipient in return. Under that standard, the distribution of counterfeit goods as samples or as gifts to cultivate a customer's goodwill might not be illegal.

The Task Force recommended further consideration of a proposal to broaden the definition of the word "traffic" in the federal trademark law so that it would explicitly include any distribution of counterfeit goods from which the distributor hopes to gain something of value from any source.

As with other laws involving intellectual property, an attempt to violate the criminal copyright statute should be a violation without regard to whether it is successful. Unlike the federal criminal trademark statute, the criminal copyright statute does not criminalize attempted violations. It is a general tenet of criminal law, however, that those who attempt to commit a crime are as morally culpable as those who succeed in doing so. As a practical matter, individuals who attempt to commit copyright crimes are disproportionately likely to have committed them in the past and to commit them again in the future (unless they have been caught and punished).

The Task Force recommended further consideration of a proposal to amend the criminal copyright statute to outlaw attempted violations.

Law enforcement officers should have access to the full range of accepted law enforcement tools when they investigate intellectual property crimes that pose a serious threat to public health or safety. A federal court may issue an order authorizing the use of a voice intercept, otherwise known as a "wiretap," in the investigation of many federal crimes, including the theft of interstate shipments, but not for intellectual property crimes. Although there are good reasons to restrict the use of wiretaps in deference to individual privacy rights, some intellectual property crimes present a more serious danger to public health or safety. Trademark violations, for instance, may involve the distribution of counterfeit goods that are defective and prone to causing widespread consumer injuries.

The Task Force recommended further consideration of a proposal to amend the Federal Wiretap Act to provide for the use of voice intercepts in investigating intellectual property crimes specifically when they threaten public health or safety.

Counterfeit and stolen intellectual property should not be permitted to flow into or out of the United States. Under current law, it is not a violation of intellectual property laws simply to import or export unauthorized copies of copyrighted works or counterfeit goods. Given the central role that international distribution plays in intellectual property crimes and the importance of not contributing in any way to intellectual property violations in other countries, the shipping of infringing products across the nation's borders should be expressly prohibited.

The Task Force recommended further consideration of a proposal to criminalize the importation and exportation of counterfeit goods and unauthorized copies of copyrighted works into and out of the United States.

Copyright law should recognize that copies of a copyrighted work are more valuable before copies of the work are released for sale to the general public. The criminal copyright statute often requires federal prosecutors to prove the retail value of the copyrighted work that has been stolen, both to establish that a criminal violation has occurred and to assess the appropriate penalty upon conviction. As explained above, however, copyrighted works that are stolen before they are released for sale lack an established retail value and yet are extraordinarily valuable. The copyright law should recognize and eliminate this tension. The Task Force recommended a proposal to assign a presumed retail value to copies of copyrighted works that have not yet been released for sale to the public.

The United States should facilitate the prosecution of individuals who are accused of intellectual property violations in another country if the violations would have been crimes under American law. Given the ease and frequency with which perpetrators of intellectual property crimes cross international borders, it is important for the United States and other nations to cooperate whenever necessary in the prosecution of these criminals. Nevertheless, under current law, the United States will not extradite an individual accused of intellectual property crimes unless (1) the United States has a treaty with the nation seeking extradition and (2) that treaty lists intellectual property crimes as a basis for extradition. This presents a significant obstacle to international cooperation because the United States has not finalized extradition treaties with many nations, and many of the treaties that the United States has concluded do not list intellectual property crimes. Therefore, the United States is often precluded from extraditing, and thus securing the extradition of, individuals accused of even the most egregious intellectual property violations.

The Task Force recommended further consideration of a proposal to permit the extradition of individuals who are accused of intellectual property violations that are criminalized under the laws of the United States and of the other nation, even in the absence of a formal extradition treaty between them.

The United States should support enhanced international enforcement of intellectual property laws. With the globalization of the economy and the rise of digital commerce, intellectual property crimes have crossed international borders with increasing frequency. The United States has signed two treaties that would facilitate international cooperation in halting some of the most egregious of these crimes: the United Nations Convention Against Transnational Organized Crime and the Council of Europe Convention on Cybercrime. The Department of Justice supports the ratification of these treaties, but the Senate has not yet voted on them.

The Task Force recommended the expeditious ratification of both treaties.

E. PREVENTION RECOMMENDATIONS

Preventing crimes from occurring in the first place is a critical component to any crime-fighting program. Publicizing successful prosecutions is an important way to deter future crimes. In addition, educational initiatives that make clear the consequences of choices must play a key role in any solution to such a pervasive and complex problem. Accordingly, the Task Force examined several public awareness and prevention issues and recommended that:

(1) The Department of Justice should develop a national program to educate students about the value of intellectual property and the consequences of committing intellectual property crimes by:

(A) Developing materials for student educational programs;

(B) Creating partnerships with non-profit educational organizations to promote public awareness regarding intellectual property crime;

(C) Developing a video to teach students about the negative consequences of intellectual property theft; and

(D) Encouraging federal prosecutors handling intellectual property crime cases throughout the nation to promote the Department of Justice's public awareness programs.

(2) The Department of Justice should educate the public about its policy prohibiting the use of peer-to-peer software on Justice Department computer systems; and

(3) The Department of Justice should promote authorized use and awareness of the FBI's new Anti-Piracy Seal to deter copyright infringement and trademark offenses.

In: DOJ Progress Report on Intellectual Property ISBN: 978-1-60741-001-0
Editor: Todd B. Parker

Chapter 10

APPENDIX B. REPORTING INTELLECTUAL PROPERTY CRIME: A GUIDE FOR VICTIMS OF COUNTERFEITING, COPYRIGHT INFRINGEMENT, AND THEFT OF TRADE SECRETS

Department of Justice

The information contained in this document has been provided by the Department of Justice's Task Force on Intellectual Property as a general guide for victims of intellectual property crime. This document is not intended to create or confer any rights, privileges, or benefits to prospective or actual witnesses or defendants. In addition, this document is not intended as a United States Department of Justice directive or as a document that has the force of law.

What Are Copyrights, Trademarks and Trade Secrets?

The United States has created enforceable rights in "intangibles" that are known as intellectual property, including copyrights, trademarks, and trade secrets. Copyright law provides federal protection against infringement of certain exclusive rights, such as reproduction and distribution, of "original works of authorship," including computer software, literary works, musical works, and motion pictures. The use of a commercial brand to identify a product is protected by trademark law, which prohibits the unauthorized use of "any word, name, symbol, or device" used by a person "to identify and distinguish his or her goods, including a unique product, from those manufactured or sold by others and to indicate the source of the goods." Finally, trade secret law protects any formula, device, or compilation of information used in a business from being disclosed without the owner's permission. Legal protection is only afforded, however, to those trade secrets that possess independent economic value and that the owner has taken reasonable measures to keep secret.

How Can Intellectual Property Be Stolen?

Intellectual property can be stolen or misappropriated in many ways. A copyrighted work may be illegally infringed by making and selling an unauthorized copy, as with infringing computer software. A trademark may be infringed by selling a good with a counterfeit mark. A trade secret may be stolen from its owner and used to benefit a competitor.

What Types of Intellectual Property Theft Constitute a Federal Crime?

Although civil remedies may provide compensation to wronged intellectual property rights holders, criminal sanctions are often warranted to ensure sufficient punishment and deterrence of wrongful activity. Congress has continually expanded and strengthened criminal laws for violations of intellectual property rights to protect innovation and ensure that egregious or persistent intellectual property violations do not merely become a standard cost of doing business for defendants. Among the most significant provisions are the following:

Counterfeit Trademarks: The Trademark Counterfeiting Act, 18 U.S.C. § 2320(a), provides penalties of up to ten years imprisonment and a $2 million fine, or twice the gross gain or gross loss, for a defendant who "intentionally traffics or attempts to traffic in goods or services and knowingly uses a counterfeit mark on or in connection with such goods or services."

Counterfeit Labeling: The counterfeit labeling provisions of 18 U.S.C. § 2318 prohibit trafficking in counterfeit labels designed to be affixed to, enclosing, or accompanying, or designed to be affixed to, phonorecords, copies of computer programs, motion pictures, audiovisual works, literary works, visual art, documentation, or packaging, as well as trafficking in counterfeit documentation or packaging for computer programs. Violations are punishable by up to 5 years imprisonment and a $250,000 fine or twice the gross gain or gross loss.

Criminal Copyright Infringement: Copyright infringement is a felony punishable by up to 3 years imprisonment and a $250,000 fine under 17 U.S.C. § 506(a) and 18 U.S.C. § 2319 when a defendant willfully reproduces or distributes at least one or more copies of phonorecords or one or more copyrighted works with a total retail value of more than $2,500 within a 180-day period. The maximum penalty rises to 5 years imprisonment if the defendant acted "for purposes of commercial advantage or private financial gain." Misdemeanor copyright infringement occurs where the value exceeds $1,000 but is equal to, or less than $2,500.

Theft of Trade Secrets: The Economic Espionage Act contains two separate provisions that criminalize the theft of trade secrets. The first provision, 18 U.S.C. § 1831(a), prohibits thefts of the trade secrets for the benefit of a foreign government or agent, and is punishable by up to 15 years imprisonment and a $500,000 fine. The second, 18 U.S.C. § 1832, prohibits thefts of commercial trade secrets, and is punishable by up to 10 years imprisonment and a $250,000 fine. The statute broadly defines the term "trade secret" to include all types of information that the owner has taken reasonable measures to keep secret and which has independent economic value.

Confidentiality: Federal law also provides special protections to victims in trade secret cases to preserve the confidentiality of the information during criminal proceedings. The statute provides that courts "shall enter such orders and take such action as may be necessary and appropriate to preserve the confidentiality of trade secrets, consistent with the requirements of the Federal Rules of Criminal and Civil Procedure, the Federal Rules of Evidence, and all other applicable laws." 18 U.S.C. § 1835.

Why Should You Report Intellectual Property Crime?

Intellectual property is an increasingly important part of the United States's economy, representing its fastest growing sector. For example, in 2002, copyright industries alone contributed approximately six percent, or $626 billion, to America's gross domestic product, and employed four percent of America's workforce, according to an economic study commissioned by the International Intellectual Property Alliance. As the Nation continues to shift from an industrial economy to an information-based economy, the assets of the country are increasingly based in intellectual property.

In recognition of this trend, the Department of Justice is waging the most aggressive campaign against the theft and counterfeiting of intellectual property in its history. The priority of criminal intellectual property investigations and prosecutions nationwide has been increased and additional resources on both the prosecutive and investigative levels have been brought to bear on the growing problem of intellectual property theft.

Effective prosecution of intellectual property crime, however, also requires substantial assistance from its victims. Because the holders of intellectual property rights are often in the best position to detect a theft, law enforcement authorities cannot act in many cases unless the crimes are reported in the first place. Once these crimes are reported, federal law enforcement authorities need to quickly identify the facts that establish jurisdiction for the potential intellectual property offenses, such as federal copyright and trademark registration information, as well as facts concerning the extent of the victim's potential loss, the nature of the theft, and possible suspects. In a digital world where evidence can disappear at the click of a mouse, swift investigation is often essential to successful intellectual property prosecutions.

Accordingly, the Department of Justice has created this handbook to facilitate the flow of critical information from victims of intellectual property crimes to law enforcement authorities. The Department of Justice's aim is to make it as easy as possible to report incidents of intellectual property crime to law enforcement authorities, including whom to call and what to tell them.

Note: The guidelines set forth below seek information that, in the experience of Department of Justice prosecutors and investigators, is useful or even critical to the successful prosecution of the most common intellectual property crimes. These guidelines are not intended to be exhaustive, nor does the presence or absence of responsive information from the victim necessarily determine the outcome of an investigation.

What Should You Do if You are Victimized?

Victims of intellectual property crime, such as counterfeiting and theft of trade secrets, often conduct internal investigations before referring matters to law enforcement. These investigations can encompass a variety of investigative steps, including interviews of witnesses, acquisition of counterfeit goods, surveillance of suspects, and examination of computers and other evidence. Victims can maximize the benefit of these independent investigative activities as follows:

1. ***Document All Investigative Steps:*** To avoid duplication of effort and retracing of steps, internal investigations should seek to create a record of all investigative steps that can later be presented to law enforcement, if necessary. If a victim company observes counterfeit goods for sale online and makes a purchase, for example, investigators should record the name of the website, the date and time of the purchase, the method of payment, and the date and manner of delivery of the goods. Any subsequent examination of the goods should then be recorded in a document that identifies the telltale characteristics of theft or counterfeiting, such as lack of a security seal, poor quality, or the like.
   Similarly, in the case of a suspected theft of trade secrets, any internal investigation or surveillance of the suspect, or a competitor believed to be using the stolen information, should be recorded in writing. A record of any interviews with suspects or witnesses should be made by tape or in writing. The pertinent confidentiality agreements, security policies, and access logs should also be gathered and maintained to facilitate review and reduce the risk of deletion or destruction.

2. ***Preserve the Evidence:*** Any physical, documentary, or digital evidence acquired in the course of an internal investigation should be preserved for later use in a legal proceeding. In the online theft example identified above, victims should printout or obtain a digital copy of the offending website and safely store any infringing goods and their packaging, which may contain valuable details of their origin. If the computer of an employee suspected of stealing trade secrets has been seized, any forensic analysis should be performed on a copy of

the data, or "digital image," to undermine claims that the evidence has been altered or corrupted.

3. ***Contact Law Enforcement Right Away:*** Victims can maximize their legal remedies for intellectual property crime by making contact with law enforcement soon after its detection. Early referral is the best way to ensure that evidence of an intellectual property crime is properly secured and that all investigative avenues, such as the execution of search warrants and possible undercover law enforcement activities, are fully explored. Communication with law enforcement authorities at the onset of suspected violations also allows a victim to coordinate civil proceedings with possible criminal enforcement. Use the reporting guides set forth later in this document to organize the information you gather and provide the necessary information to your law enforcement contact.

How Can You Assist Law Enforcement?

Prosecutions of intellectual property crime often depend on cooperation between victims and law enforcement. Indeed, without information sharing from intellectual property rights holders, prosecutors can neither discern the trends that suggest the most effective overall enforcement strategies, nor meet the burden of proving the theft of intellectual property in a specific case. The following seeks to provide guidance concerning the types of assistance that may be offered by victims of intellectual property theft to law enforcement authorities.

Identify Stolen Intellectual Property: Just as in cases involving traditional theft, such as a burglary or shoplifting, victims of intellectual property theft may – and often must – assist law enforcement in the identification of stolen property. Thus, law enforcement may call upon a victim representative or expert to examine items obtained during an investigation to determine their origin or authenticity. In a copyright infringement or trademark investigation, for example, an author or software company may be called upon to analyze CDs or other media that appear to be counterfeit, while a victim representative in a theft of trade secret case may be asked to review documents or computer source code. Prosecutors may later seek expert testimony from the victims at trial.

In certain investigations, law enforcement agents also may request a victim's presence during the execution of a search warrant to help the agents identify specific items to be seized. In those circumstances, the victim's activities will be strictly limited to those directed by supervising law enforcement agents.

Share the Results of Internal Investigations or Civil Lawsuits: As with any suspected crime, victims may provide law enforcement with information gathered as a result of internal investigations into instances of intellectual property theft. In addition, unless the proceedings or information have been ordered sealed by a court, victims may generally provide law enforcement with any evidence or materials developed in civil intellectual property enforcement actions, including court pleadings, deposition testimony, documents, and written discovery responses.

Participate in Law Enforcement Task Forces: Federal, state, and local law enforcement agencies and prosecutors all over the country have formed task forces to combat computer and intellectual property crime and to promote information sharing between government and industry. The United States Secret Service, for example, has created Electronic Crimes Task Forces in 13 cities, and the Federal Bureau of Investigation has founded more than 60 "Infragard" chapters around the country. In addition, many areas have "high-tech crime" task forces that investigate intellectual property theft. Members of the intellectual property industry are encouraged to participate in these organizations to establish law enforcement contacts that will enable these members to quickly respond to incidents of intellectual property and other crime. (Information on joining these organizations is available online at www.ectaskforce.org and www.infragard.net*)*.

Contributions of Funds, Property, or Services: Donating funds, property, or services to federal law enforcement authorities can raise potential legal and ethical issues that must be addressed on a case-by-case basis. In general, federal law places limitations on contributions to law enforcement authorities.

If you or your company have become the victim of a copyright infringement or counterfeit trademark offensc, please fill out the information indicated below and contact a federal law enforcement official to report the offense.

CHECKLIST FOR REPORTING A COPYRIGHT INFRINGEMENT OR COUNTERFEIT TRADEMARK OFFENSE

Background and Contact Information:

1. Victim's Name:
2. Primary Address:
3. Nature of Business:
4. Contact:

Phone: Fax:
Email: Pager/Mobile:

Description of the Intellectual Property

5. Describe the copyrighted material or trademark (e.g., title of copyrighted work, identity of logo):
6. Is the copyrighted work or trademark registered with the United States Copyright Office or the United States Patent and Trademark Office? ___ YES ___NO

a. If so, please provide the following:
   (i) Registration Date:
   (ii) Registration Number:
   (iii) Do you have a copy of the certificate of registration?
   (iv) Has the work or mark been the subject of a previous civil or criminal enforcement action? If so, please provide a general description.

b. If not, state if and when you intend to register:

7. What is the approximate retail value of the copyrighted work or trademarked good?

Description of the Intellectual Property Crime

8. Describe how the theft or counterfeiting was discovered:
9. Do you have any examination reports of the infringing or counterfeit goods? ___YES ___NO. (If so, please provide those reports to the law enforcement official).

10. Describe the scope of the theft or counterfeiting operation, including the following information:
    (a) Estimated quantity of illegal distribution:
    (b) Estimated time period of illegal distribution:
    (c) Is the illegal distribution national or international? Which states or countries?
11. Identify where the theft or counterfeiting occurred, and describe the location:
12. Identify the name(s) or location(s) of possible suspects, including the following information:
    Name (Suspect #1):
    Phone number:
    Email address:
    Physical address:
    Current employer, if known:
    Reason for suspicion:
    Name (Suspect #2):
    Phone number:
    Email address:
    Physical address:
    Current employer, if known:
    Reason for suspicion:
13. If the distribution of infringing or counterfeit goods involves the Internet (e.g., World Wide Web, FTP, email, chat rooms), identify the following:
    (a) The type of Internet theft:
    (b) Internet address, including linking sites (domain name, URL, IP address, email):
    (c) Login or password for site:
    (d) Operators of site, if known:
14. If you have conducted an internal investigation into the theft or counterfeiting activities, please describe any evidence acquired:

Civil Enforcement Proceedings

15. Has a civil enforcement action been filed against the suspects identified above? ___YES ___NO
    (a) If so, identify the following:

(i) Name of court and case number:
(ii) Date of filing:
(iii) Names of attorneys:
(iv) Status of case:

(b) If not, is a civil action contemplated? What type and when?

16. Please provide any information concerning the suspected crime not described above that you believe might assist law enforcement.

CHECKLIST FOR REPORTING A THEFT OF TRADE SECRETS OFFENSE[1]

If you or your company have become the victim of a theft of trade secrets offense, please fill out the information indicated below and contact a federal law enforcement official to report the offense. An insert with contact information for law enforcement officials in your area should be included at the end of this guide.

NOTE ON CONFIDENTIALITY: Federal law provides that courts "shall enter such orders and take such action as may be necessary and appropriate to preserve the confidentiality of trade secrets, consistent with the requirements of the Federal Rules of Criminal and Civil Procedure, the Federal Rules of Evidence, and all other applicable laws." 18 U.S .C. § 1835. Prosecutors utilizing any of the information set forth below will generally request the court to enter an order to preserve the status of the information as a trade secret and prevent its unnecessary and harmful disclosure.

Background and Contact Information

1. Victim's Name:
2. Primary Location and Address:
3. Nature of Primary Business:
4. Law Enforcement Contact:

Phone: Fax:
Email: Pager/Mobile:

Description of the Trade Secret

5. Generally describe the trade secret (e.g., source code, formula):

Provide an estimated value of the trade secret identifying ONE of the methods and indicating ONE of the ranges listed below:

Method

- Cost to Develop the Trade Secret;
- Acquisition Cost (identify date and source of acquisition); or
- Fair Market Value if sold.

Estimated Value

- Under $50,000;
- Between $50,000 and $100,000;
- Between $100,000 and $1 million;
- Between $1 million and $5 million; or
- Over $5 million.

Identify a person knowledgeable about valuation, including that person's contact information:

General Physical Measures Taken to Protect the Trade Secret

6. Describe the general physical security precautions taken by the company, such as fencing the perimeter of the premises, visitor control systems, using alarming or self-locking doors, or hiring security personnel.
7. Has the company established physical barriers to prevent unauthorized viewing or access to the trade secret, such as "Authorized Personnel Only" signs at access points? (See below if computer stored trade secret.) ___YES ___NO

8. Does the company require sign in/out procedures for access to and return of trade secret materials? ___YES ___NO
9. Are employees required to wear identification badges? ___YES ___ NO
10. Does the company have a written security policy? ___YES ___NO
    (a) How are employees advised of the security policy?
    (b) Are employees required to sign a written acknowledgment of the security policy? ___YES ___NO
    (c) Identify the person most knowledgeable about matters relating to the security policy, including title and contact information.
11. How many employees have access to the trade secret?
12. Was access to the trade secret limited to a "need to know" basis? ___YES ___NO

Confidentiality and Non-Disclosure Agreements

13. Does the company enter into confidentiality and non-disclosure agreements with employees and third-parties concerning the trade secret? ___YES ___NO
14. Has the company established and distributed written confidentiality policies to all employees? ___YES ___NO
15. Does the company have a policy for advising company employees regarding the company's trade secrets? ___YES ___NO

Computer-Stored Trade Secrets

16. If the trade secret is computer source code or other computer-stored information, how is access regulated (e.g., are employees given unique user names and passwords)?
17. If the company stores the trade secret on a computer network, is the network protected by a firewall? ___YES ___NO
18. Is remote access permitted into the computer network? ___YES ___NO
19. Is the trade secret maintained on a separate computer server? ___YES ____NO

20. Does the company prohibit employees from bringing outside computer programs or storage media to the premises? ___YES ___NO
21. Does the company maintain electronic access records such as computer logs? ___YES ___NO

Document Control

22. If the trade secret consisted of documents, were they clearly marked "CONFIDENTIAL" or "PROPRIETARY"? ___YES ___NO
23. Describe the document control procedures employed by the company, such as limiting access and sign in/out policies.
24. Was there a written policy concerning document control procedures and, if so, how were employees advised of it? ___YES ___NO
25. Identify the person most knowledgeable about the document control procedures, including title and contact information.

Employee Controls

26. Are new employees subject to a background investigation? ___YES ___NO
27. Does the company hold "exit interviews" to remind departing employees of their obligation not to disclose trade secrets? ___YES ___NO

Description of the Theft of Trade Secret

28. Identify the name(s) or location(s) of possible suspects, including the following information:
    Name (Suspect #1):
    Phone number:
    Email address:
    Physical address:
    Employer:
    Reason for suspicion:

Name (Suspect #2): Phone number:
Email address:
Physical address:
Employer:
Reason for suspicion:

29. Was the trade secret stolen to benefit a third party, such as a competitor or another business? ___YES ___NO
If so, identify that business and its location:
30. Do you have any information that the theft of the trade secret was committed to benefit a foreign government or instrumentality of a foreign government? ___YES ___NO
If so, identify the foreign government and describe that information.
31. If the suspect is a current or former employee, describe all confidentiality and non-disclosure agreements in effect.
32. Identify any physical locations tied to the theft of the trade secret, such as where it may be currently stored or used.
33. If you have conducted an internal investigation into the theft or ounterfeiting activities, please describe any evidence acquired:

Civil Enforcement Proceedings

34. Has a civil enforcement action been filed against the suspects identified above? ___YES ___NO
   (a) If so, identify the following:
      (i) Name of court and case number:
      (ii) Date of filing:
      (iii) Names of attorneys:
      (iv) Status of case:
   (b) If not, is a civil action contemplated?
   What type and when?
35. Please provide any information concerning the suspected crime not described above that you believe might assist law enforcement.

End Notes

[1] Special thanks to Deputy District Attorney James Sibley, Santa Clara District Attorney's Office, for providing this checklist.

INDEX

C

F

G

H

I

J

K

L

M

N

O

Q

R

S

T

U

V

W